Contents

SECTION THREE: CONTINGENCY PLANNING

RESOURCES

Planning and Decision Making

by:

Jane Smith

BLACKWELL
Business

THE
OPEN
LEARNING
FOUNDATION

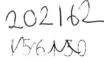

Copyright © Open Learning Foundation Enterprises Ltd 1996

First published 1996

Blackwell Publishers Ltd
108 Cowley Road
Oxford OX4 1JF, UK

238 Main Street
Cambridge, Massachusetts 02142, USA

Every effort has been made to trace all copyright owners of material used in this book but if any have been inadvertently overlooked the publishers will be pleased to make necessary arrangements at the first opportunity.

British Library Cataloguing-in-Publication Data
A CIP catalogue record for this book is available from the British Library

Library of Congress Cataloging-in-Publication Data
A catalogue record for this book is available from the Library of Congress

ISBN 0-631-19675-7

Printed in Great Britain by Alden Press

This book is printed on acid-free paper

Foreword

BTEC is committed to helping people of any age to acquire and maintain the up-to-date and relevant knowledge, understanding and skills they need for success in current or future employment.

These aims are greatly enhanced by this series of open learning books for the new BTEC HND and HNC in Business Studies.

These books will provide more students with the opportunity to achieve a widely recognised national qualification in business by allowing flexible study patterns combined with an innovative approach to learning.

Our active involvement in a partnership with the Open Learning Foundation and Blackwell Publishers ensures that each book comprehensively covers the specific learning outcomes needed for a module in this Higher National programme.

Acknowledgments

Author
Jane Smith

Open Learning Editor: Jane Edmonds

For the Open Learning Foundation:
Director of Programmes: Leslie Mapp
Design and Production: Stephen Moulds
Text Editor: Paul Stirner
Academic Co-ordinator: Glyn Roberts (Bradford & Ilkley
                                                    Community College)
Academic Reviewers: Martin Gibson (University of Central
                                          Lancashire)

                                          Bob McClelland (Liverpool John Moores
                                          University)

The Open Learning Foundation wishes to acknowledge the support
of Bradford & Ilkley Community College during the preparation of
this workbook.

For BTEC
Diane Billam: Director of Products and Quality Division
John Edgar: Consultant
Françoise Seacroft: Manager of Futures Department
Mike Taylor: Deputy Head of Department of Service Sector
                        Management, University of Brighton

For Blackwell Publishers
Editorial Director: Philip Carpenter
Senior Commissioning Editor: Tim Goodfellow
Production Manager: Pam Park
Development Editors: Richard Jackman and Catriona King
Pre-production Manager: Paul Stringer
Sub-editorial team: First Class Publishing
Reviewers: Howard Brown (West Herts College)
                    Frank Valentine (University of West of England)

Copyright acknowledgments

The Mind Map shown in figure 3.2 in section 2, session 3 was created by Vanda North using the concept of Mind Mapping devised by Tony Buzan. This example first appeared in *The Mind Map Book* (2nd edn, 1995, p.126) published by BBC Worldwide. The publishers are grateful to Tony Buzan, Vanda North and BBC Worldwide for permission to reproduce this map.

Introduction

Welcome to this workbook for the BTEC module Planning and Decision Making.

This is a book specifically designed for use by students studying on BTEC Higher National programmes in Business, Business and Finance, Business and Marketing and Business and Personnel. However, it can be also used by people who wish to learn about this aspect of business.

How to use the workbook

Please feel free to:

- write notes in the margins

- underline and highlight important words or phrases.

As you work through this module, you will find activities have been built in. These are designed to make you stop to think and answer questions.

There are four types of activities.

Memory and recall These are straightforward tests of how much text you are able to remember.

Self-assessed tasks (SATs) These are used to test your understanding of the text you are studying or to apply the principles and practices learnt to a related problem.

Exercises These are open-ended questions that can be used as a basis for classroom or group debate. If you do not belong to a study group, use the exercises to think through issues raised by the text.

Assignments These are tasks set for students studying at a BTEC centre which would normally require a written answer to be looked at by your tutor. If you are not following a course at college, the assignments are still a useful way of developing and testing your understanding of the module.

There are answer boxes provided below each activity in this module. Use these boxes to summarise your answers and findings. If you need more space, use the margins of the book or separate sheets of paper to make notes and write a full answer.

SAT:
allow 10 mins

Managing tasks and solving problems ✔

EXAMPLE ACTIVITY

As an 'icebreaker' try this exercise.

Within the objectives that form a company's strategic plan are policies that can often become the hallmark of that organisation. Think of a company whose reputation is founded on one specific trading policy.

Commentary...

Two good examples from the high street are Marks and Spencer and the Body Shop. The good reputation of M&S is firmly linked to its high quality products and its 'no quibbling' exchange or refund policy. Similarly, the Body Shop is renowned for only selling products that have not been tested on animals.

The emphasis of the workbook is to provide you with tasks that relate to the general operating environment of business. The work that you do on these tasks enables you to develop your BTEC common skills and a skills chart is provided at the end of this introduction for you to note your practice of each skill. One sheet is probably not enough, so cut this sheet out and photocopy it when you require new sheets.

Aims of the workbook

This workbook is concerned with devloping students' understanding of organisational planning and decision processes and the constraints and uncertainties within which they take place. It provides a framework for the student to apply the techniques of decision making and contingency planning.

The book has three sections which are designed to cover the learning outcomes (as shown in bold in the boxes below) for this core module. These are as given in the BTEC publication (code 02–104–4) on the Higher National programmes in Business Studies. Where appropriate, BTEC's suggested content may be reordered within the sections of this book.

SECTION ONE: THE PLANNING FRAMEWORK

On completion of this section, you should be able to:

> ◗ **examine the process of organisation planning**

> ◗ **analyse the relationship between corporate, functional and individual objectives**

> ◗ **evaluate objectives of different business functions within the overall organisational plan**

Content

Effective planning: the importance of planning and the types of plans used in organisations; managerial implementation of plans; elements of effective plans; team and individual participation; the planning cycle and the control loop.

Types of plan: operational and strategic plans; the complexities of strategic planning; the use of budgeting to create structured and precise plans; plans for individuals and performance appraisal systems; project planning to achieve specific purposes within set times; defining objectives.

Ideas into action: keeping the organisation on course with a shared mission; developing a vision to start the planning process; the development of policies within the framework of an organisation's objectives; maintaining strategies in multidivisional companies; differences in planning in large organisations, small businesses and in the public sector.

Planning for change: the reasons why businesses are forced to plan for change; the six main external influences on organisational planning; the internal characteristics that help or hinder company development; analysing company strengths and opportunities; assessing the risks associated with plans for change.

SECTION TWO: DECISION MAKING

On completion of this section, you should be able to:

> ▶ **examine and explain the process of decision making by individuals in organisations**

> ▶ **identify and evaluate the organisational factors which affect decision making**

> ▶ **select and use decision making techniques**

Content

What decision making involves: the role of effective decision making in business; types of decisions to be made and the associated means of implementation; decision-making styles and selecting the best approach for given situations; the key steps in making decisions.

Obtaining information for decisions: the need for high-quality information for effective decision making; selecting appropriate information; sources of relevant information; the relationship between organisational structures and information flows; computerised communication networks.

Creative approach: using creativity to find new solutions; the characteristics of the creative organisation; fostering and encouraging creativity; beliefs and behaviour that underpin creative management styles; techniques for creative decision making.

Choosing between options: the criteria that can be used to evaluate options - feasibility, acceptability and risk; the factors that influence decision makers' personal perceptions; techniques used to select the most promising option.

SECTION THREE: CONTINGENCY PLANNING

On completion of this section, you should be able to:

▶ **identify and evaluate how organisations plan for contingencies**

▶ **compare and contrast pragmatic as compared to planned approaches to contingencies**

▶ **identify and evaluate alternative strategies for coping with risk**

▶ **prepare and evaluate contingency plans**

Content

Identifying contingencies: the nature and purposes of contingency plans; the benefits of a planned approach over ad hoc reaction; building scenarios and forecasting to facilitate planning; approaches to contingency planning and assessing the organisational constraints on implementation; recognising contingencies.

Coping with risk: analysing risk in terms of possible outcomes or contingencies; objective and subjective probability; how to identify and describe types of decision model; constructing decision trees; sensitivity analysis and dealing with contingencies.

In working through the BTEC Higher National programme in Business Studies, you will practice the following BTEC common skills:

Managing and developing self	✔
Working with and relating to others	✔
Communicating	✔
Managing tasks and solving problems	✔
Applying numeracy	✔
Applying technology	✔
Applying design and creativity	✔

You will practise most of these skills in working through this module.

Recommended reading

Cashmore, C. and Lyall, R., 1991, *Business Information Systems and Strategies*, Englewood Cliffs, NJ, Prentice Hall.

Cook, S. and Slack, N., 1991, *Making Management Decisions*, 2nd edn, Englewood Cliffs, NJ, Prentice Hall.

Drucker, P. F., 1994, *The Practice of Management*, London, Butterworth Heinemann.

Garratt, Bob, 1994, *Creating a Learning Organisation*, 2nd edn, Harper Collins.

Glew, M., Watts, M. and Wells, R., 1979, *The Business Organisation and its Environment*, London, Heinemann Educational.

Johnson, G. and Scholes, G., 1993, *Exploring Corporate Strategy*, Englewood Cliffs, NJ, Prentice Hall.

Kanter, R. M., 1985, *The Change Masters*, London, Allen & Unwin.

Mintzberg, H., 1994, *The Rise and Fall of Strategic Planning*, Englewood Cliffs, NJ, Prentice Hall.

Richardson, W. and Richardson, R., 1992, *Business Planning: An Approach to Strategic Management*, 2nd edn, London, Pitman Publishing

Schwenk, C. R., 1988, *The Essence of Strategic Decision Making*, Lexington Books.

Name

Module

BTEC Skill	Activity No./Date	Activity No./Date	Activity No./Date	Activity No./Date	Activity No./Date
Managing and developing self					
Working with and relating to others					
Communicating					
Managing tasks and solving problems					
Applying numeracy					
Applying technology					
Applying design and creativity					

The Planning Framework

Effective planning

WHY PLANNING IS
IMPORTANT

MANAGEMENT STYLES

THE FEATURES OF
EFFECTIVE PLANS

THE PLANNING CYCLE

THE CONTROL LOOP

Objectives

After participating in this session, you should be able to:

▶ identify the benefits of systematic planning for individuals and organisations

▶ explore a variety of management styles and state which ones are more conducive to effective planning

▶ describe the characteristic features of successful plans

▶ describe how plans at different levels of the organisation link and support each other

▶ identify the different stages of the 'control loop' and explain how these combine to control an organisation's output.

In working through this session, you will practise the following BTEC common skills:

Managing and developing self	✔
Working with and relating to others	✔
Communicating	✔
Managing tasks and solving problems	✔
Applying numeracy	
Applying technology	
Applying design and creativity	

Why planning is important

The business that is not being purposely led in a clear direction which is understood by its people is not going to survive, and all of history shows that this is the case.

John Harvey-Jones, 1988, *Making it Happen*, Fontana

We all know that some people and organisations always succeed while others never seem to do quite so well. Many people put success down to 'luck', especially those unsuccessful individuals who persist in reflecting on their 'bad luck' rather than on their not too effective or non-existent plans. Whether we are talking about a swimming gala, an international company, a newsagent's shop, a charity or a country, it could be argued that good planning is the single factor which makes one organisation, individual or project more successful than the next.

Planning is the most basic – and some would say the most important – of all management functions. If an organisation is to be effective, everyone involved must know where they are going and how they are expected to arrive there. Planning bridges the gap from where the organisation is now to where it wants to be. It makes it possible for organisational development and change to occur and for businesses to achieve their desired goals.

The development of an organisation and the quality of the work it produces also depend on effective decision making. This process enables managers to:

- select their goals and objectives

- move their work on, to achieve their objectives and tasks

- gain people's commitment to the organisation's purpose.

Unfortunately, plans and decisions rarely work out as managers hope they will. The business environment is changing so fast that unforeseen events occur to affect their carefully thought-out ideas and decisions. So they use **contingency planning** – a technique for reducing uncertainty in strategic and operational planning. Contingency plans are made in preparation for the more likely major factors which will seriously affect an organisation and the achievement of its long-term success.

THE FEATURES OF PLANS

Figure 1.1 shows an extract from plans made by a manufacturing company and gives some idea of the kinds of statements that businesses make in their plans. It also helps to explain some of the language of planning.

Goal: To identify the changing needs of our paying customers and improve the whole process of satisfying those needs from first customer contact through to aftersales service.

Objective 1: To improve the customer service process and achieve a stronger focus on customer satisfaction.

Actions:
Integrate the Customer Service and Product Development departments.
Provide telephone skills training for Customer Service staff.
Analyse the sources and patterns of customer complaints and adopt a solution based approach.

Targets:
Training complete in six months.
Repeat complaints reduced by 50% in six months and eliminated in one year.

Objective 2: To identify and meet customers' current and future needs.

Actions:
Research customer requirements.
Develop systems to refine the links between sales and customer service.

Targets:
Analysis completed in six months.
Improve customer satisfaction rating by 3% in one year.

FIGURE 1.1: *Extract from company plans.*

ACTIVITY 1

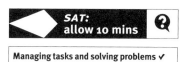

SAT:
allow 10 mins

Managing tasks and solving problems ✓

Refer to the extract from a plan shown in figure 1.1 to answer the following questions in your own words.

(a) What is the overall purpose of the above plan?

(b) What are the two main ways in which this main purpose will be achieved?

(c) How will the organisation know when customers are happier with the standard of the services provided?

Commentary...

Now check how far your responses match ours. Note that we have tried to 'translate' the rather formal planning jargon into more everyday language.

The overall purpose of the plan is to improve the organisation's ability to identify and satisfy the needs of its customers. This purpose will be achieved

    (a) by raising the standard of customer service and

    (b) by meeting customer needs more efficiently.

The organisation will know that customers are happier with the standard of the services provided when customer complaints are reduced and its customer satisfaction rating is improved.

THE BENEFITS OF PLANNING

Many different types of plans exist to provide specific outcomes or benefits for the organisation as a whole and for groups or individuals within it. The main ones that we consider here are: strategic plans and operational plans.

Strategic plans reflect the decisions that organisations have made about their future activities and long-term goals. Traditionally, they cover a period of about three to five years.

Operational plans are concerned with how the different functions of the organisation will contribute to the organisation's overall goals and objectives. The period which they cover is usually about one year.

In addition, there are **project plans, business plans, personal development plans** and **action plans**.

Later, we look at **contingency plans** which can be attached to any type of plan. These are created to cope with any current problems, either circumstantial or environmental, which endanger the organisation's ability to achieve its goals and objectives.

A **plan** is an unambiguous guidance framework that helps to organise people and align their efforts towards the same goals. Without a clear plan, there is a risk of divergence or dissent.

Having said all that, it would be wrong to imagine that, once made, plans must be set in 'tablets of stone'. It is important to review them regularly in the light of changing circumstances and to adapt them if necessary. It's like setting off on a journey from Edinburgh to Liverpool. If you are wise, you will plan your route before you set off, having found out as much as you can about weather conditions, the state of the roads and potential traffic problems. However, if you find that conditions change during the journey, you don't stick blindly to your original plan; you will adapt it to meet the new situation.

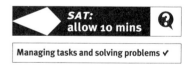

Managing tasks and solving problems ✔

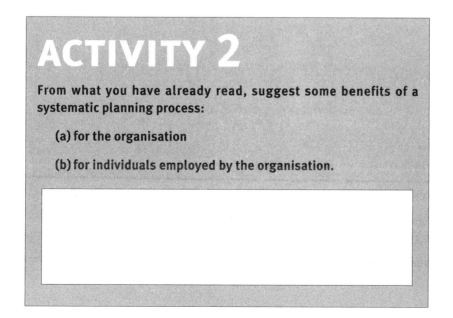

ACTIVITY 2

From what you have already read, suggest some benefits of a systematic planning process:

(a) **for the organisation**

(b) **for individuals employed by the organisation.**

Commentary...

You may have noted some of the following benefits.

Plans help organisations to:

- define their future direction

- decide how they are going to achieve their goals

- monitor their progress towards their goals.

Plans help individuals to:

- understand the objectives of the organisation

- understand how they can contribute to achieving specified goals

- ensure that they align their efforts with people in other teams or departments.

Management styles

The success of an organisation depends almost entirely on the commitment of the workforce to achieving its goals and objectives. The extent to which people feel committed depends both on how those goals and objectives have been arrived at, and the way in which plans are put into action. Experience has shown that some management styles are more successful than others, and organisations can learn much from analysing the relative effectiveness of different approaches to decision making and planning.

An important aspect of making sure that people can give of their best is to ensure they understand:

- the goals and objectives of the organisation as a whole, and

- how they can make a contribution towards achieving these.

For example, during the 1980s, ICL managed to turn a pre-tax loss of nearly £50 million into a profit of £149 million in the space of eight years. The company ascribed much of this success to the goals that were established during this period in consultation with its managers.

An organisation's goals need to be translated into the work that each department carries out and then into detailed performance objectives for managers, teams and team members.

In some organisations, the manager is expected to set objectives for his or her staff and communicate this to the people concerned. The individuals within the team may have the opportunity to discuss the objectives set for them or they may be excluded from this process. The overall process is very much a top-down one.

Some organisations adopt an alternative approach and encourage employees at all levels to participate in objective setting. Involving people can lead to better planning because it draws in the people who know most. It also increases their commitment to decisions that directly affect them and raises levels of job satisfaction.

The continuum shown in figure 1.2 is a useful way of ranking management styles.

FIGURE 1.2: *The management style continuum.*

The **autocratic style** is the 'top-down' approach, where leaders or managers make all the decisions and plans by themselves. They then pass these down through the hierarchy to first line managers and the workers who have to implement them.

The **consultative style** describes the approach whereby managers discuss problems and issues with their subordinates, before deciding on a course of action that may, or may not, reflect their views.

The **participative style** is the 'bottom-up' approach where everyone in the organisation is involved to some extent in planning, decision making and problem solving.

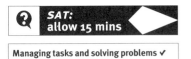

Managing tasks and solving problems ✓

ACTIVITY 3

Read what these three managers have to say about their styles of management and identify which style – autocratic, consultative or participatory – best describes each approach.

My staff are very busy with their own jobs. I see my role as developing the structure of the business, finding new markets and communicating with customers. I always keep people informed and ask them for their views and ideas when the issues concern them. But it's not always possible to hold a meeting every time I have to make a decision.

Angela Hardy, director of a small publishing company

I like to think very carefully before making important decisions. I know what's best ... I look after my people and always have their best interests in mind when I make decisions that affect them. I make a point of letting everyone know ... so I send at least two memos to section managers every week.

Steve Morris, manager in charge of a light engineering firm

We believe in devolving responsibility to the lowest possible level ... It is company policy to involve everyone in generating and implementing ideas. After all, it's the workforce who are closest to the customer – it stands to reason that they are going to know best how to improve communications or services.

Eric Dunn, district manager in an electricity company

Commentary...

If you have a part-time job or work experience placement, the approaches described above may already be familiar to you.

Angela Hardy involves the workforce up to a point, but always takes final responsibility for decisions. The style is consultative. Steve Morris does not seem to consult at all, he takes all the decisions by himself. The style is autocratic. With Eric Dunn, responsibility is shared as far as possible with the workforce. The style is participative.

ACTIVITY 4

EXERCISE:
allow 15 mins

Working with and relating to others ✓

Managing tasks and solving problems ✓

Following on from the previous activity, consider the styles of managers you know now or have known in the past and try to identify the category into which they fall. Working in small groups, suggest some advantages and disadvantages of the different approaches. Summarise the conclusions of your group in the box below.

Style	Advantages	Disadvantages
Autocratic		
Consultative		
Participative		

Commentary...

Where senior managers hold on to most of the responsibility for making policies and plans, the main advantages are that:

- decisions can be taken rapidly
- lower level managers and subordinates have more time to allocate to performing their tasks.

However:

- the resources of the whole workforce are not used to the full
- subordinates are not always fully committed to someone else's plans.

When top management always consult before identifying objectives and making plans:

- subordinates are given the chance to air their views
- they know what managers have in mind before these ideas become a reality.

However:

- people may become frustrated if their ideas are not taken into account
- it takes a long time to canvass opinions informally.

Where everyone shares responsibility for what happens:

- the whole workforce – managers and subordinates alike – are fully committed to plans that are made
- the organisation will have utilised its full range of human resources.

However:

- involving everyone fully takes a long time
- minor issues may become exaggerated out of proportion.

A word of caution: the three styles are intended as caricatures with the purpose of underlining the differences between the different types. In reality, few managers use a single approach the whole time, although some may favour one rather than the others. You often find managers who are autocratic, consultative and participative in different situations. The skill is in using the approach that best suits the circumstances at the time:

- An autocratic style is most useful for routine or urgent decisions.

- A consultative style is most useful where managers need to find out what people think but cannot necessarily put these ideas into practice.

- A participative style is useful when managers want the whole workforce involved in making decisions, planning and putting plans into action.

RECALL:
allow 5 mins

What is planning at the corporate level usually called?

What is planning within the different functions or departments usually called?

The features of effective plans

We have discussed that planning takes place at both strategic and operational levels within an organisation. You may also come across 'project plans', 'action plans', 'marketing plans', 'training plans', 'personal development plans', and so on. All these different types of plan usually have a number of elements in common:

- goals

- objectives

- strategies

- tactics or tasks.

People in business and authors of management texts use these terms in a variety of ways. Some say that objectives are more precise than goals, others exactly the opposite.

> **Goals are the intention behind decisions or actions ... an objective is a goal expressed in a form by which its attainment can be measured.**

Henry Mintzberg, 1983, *Power in and around Organisations*, Prentice Hall

In the material below, we have included some definitions of these terms that are commonly used in private and public sector businesses in the UK. But proceed with caution because it sometimes seems that the terms have as many interpretations as there are planners!

GOALS

A goal is more than a dream or an aspiration – it's a dream being acted upon. Nothing happens, and no forward steps can be taken until goals are established. Without goals, individuals, groups and whole organisations just wander through their lives and their work. They stumble along, never knowing where they are heading, so it's not surprising if they never get anywhere.

Here are two examples of goals set by an airline:

- to secure a leading share of air travel business world-wide

- to provide overall superior service and good value for money.

Goals, then, are general statements of aims or purposes.

OBJECTIVES

Objectives are statements of what the organisation, group or individual has to achieve in the period covered by the plan. The choice of objectives is an essential part of the decision-making process because they point the way towards future courses of action. Sometimes you will see objectives that are implicit and generalised – in this case, they are probably no more than detailed statements of intent. If, however, they are made formal and explicit they will highlight the comparative importance of various activities and provide meaningful criteria for evaluating performance.

Other terms for objectives are goals, ends, purposes, targets and quotas. But, whatever they are called, they specify results and outcomes that someone believes are worth achieving. They can be long term (several years), medium term (one or two years) or short term (months, days or hours).

Many groups and individuals clarify their objectives by ensuring they are **SMART** – specific, measurable, attainable, realistic and time limited:

- **specific** – so there's no doubt about what outcome is expected

- **measurable** – by cost, quality, quantity or a mixture of these

- **attainable** – because if they are not attainable in the time allocated, they are a waste of time

- **realistic** – people are not motivated if they have to work on something they know they cannot achieve

- **time limited** – so they are focused and are about moving forward over a set period of time, at the end of which the results can be measured.

SAT:
allow 10 mins

Managing tasks and solving problems ✔

ACTIVITY 5

Here are some of the airline's objectives:

1. to excel in anticipating and responding to customer needs

2. to achieve profits of over £200 million in the year ending April 1996 after all charges

3. to reduce delays in baggage handling by 10 per cent by November 1996

4. to expand our business by creating market alliances.

Which ones are SMART? Explain the reasons for your answer.

Commentary...

Only objectives 2 and 3 may be SMART because they are specific, measurable and time limited. However, we do not have enough information to judge whether they are attainable or realistic. The other two objectives are general statements of intent and are not SMART.

STRATEGIES

This term can be particularly confusing because it is open to a number of interpretations. Inexperienced planners sometimes believe that only strategic plans can have strategies. But this is not the case – in fact all types of plans can and do include strategies.

Strategies define the broad categories or types of action that are required to achieve the objectives. Depending on the level of the plan, strategies may involve restructuring, developing systems, refurbishing office space, acquiring equipment, managing resources, coaching and carrying out market research.

Here are some strategies outlined by the airline:

- Our strategy is to expand our core business by creating market alliances where possible and by investing in other airlines.

- We will positively influence the opinion held by key customer groups through sustained pro-active public relations campaigns, using media relations, sponsorship, external events and promotions.

TACTICS

Sometimes strategies are further broken down into tactics – the individual actions and tasks that will be required to implement the strategies. They are often allocated to identified groups or individuals and may include specified time-scales for completion.

The airline defines its tactics as follows:

- During the financial year 1995–96, the marketing group will agree a marketing partnership with two other airline services.

- The company shall set aside an investment fund of £20 million to acquire a stake in another airline.

ACTIVITY 6

Draw up a personal action plan for achieving a goal that is important for you. Make sure that your plan includes the following:

- ● a goal or goals

- ● clear, timed and measurable objectives

- ● strategies for achieving the objectives.

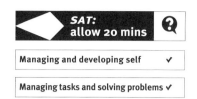

SAT:
allow 20 mins

Managing and developing self ✔

Managing tasks and solving problems ✔

Commentary...

Here is an example of an action plan that many people can relate to.

Goal: to look better and feel healthier.

Objectives:

1. to lose half a stone by Christmas

2. to wear an outfit that is one size smaller than my current size at my Christmas party.

Strategies:

- Cut out all biscuits, crisps, cakes and other fattening snacks.

- Eat more vegetables and fruit.

- Get up early enough to have a healthy, filling breakfast.

- Reduce alcohol intake – substitute with low-calorie drinks.

- Exercise three times a week.

The planning cycle

There are many ways of drawing up and presenting organisational plans. What matters is that people at all levels – from the board of directors to front-line employees – work together on plans that are appropriate to them and support the overall goals and policies of the organisation.

An effective planning process will incorporate a **'cascade' principle** like the one described here.

- A vision or policy and overall goals for the organisation are created at the top.

- The broad goals flow down to the next level, where the different departments or functions set objectives and identify how they can achieve them. Sometimes, individual departments and units produce their own business plans which set out in detail how they intend to contribute to the organisation's long-term goals.

- If necessary, goals are specified at the lower levels and broken down still further so that separate sections or teams can understand and recognise their part in the process that makes up organisational success.

- Individuals know (because they have plans that specify their personal objectives or targets) what they have to contribute, day to day.

However, as you have seen, some organisations are also starting to recognise the benefits of a planning process which is not just 'top-down', but incorporates the input of all staff at all levels of planning.

Figure 1.3 illustrates the hierarchy of plans and shows how plans at the different levels should be linked and mutually supportive. The two-way arrows illustrate the negotiation that must take place between the levels if the plans are to be meaningful and successful. The required interaction between groups and individuals at the same level is not shown.

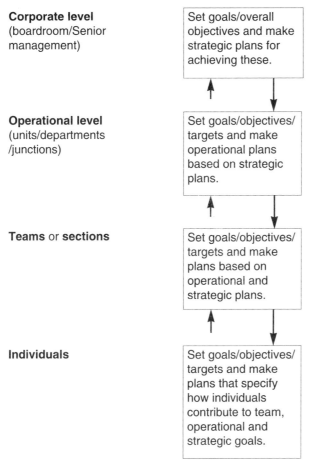

Corporate level
(boardroom/Senior management)

> Set goals/overall objectives and make strategic plans for achieving these.

Operational level
(units/departments /junctions)

> Set goals/objectives/ targets and make operational plans based on strategic plans.

Teams or **sections**

> Set goals/objectives/ targets and make plans based on operational and strategic plans.

Individuals

> Set goals/objectives/ targets and make plans that specify how individuals contribute to team, operational and strategic goals.

FIGURE 1.3: *A hierarchy of plans.*

The control loop

Planning becomes a useless and demoralising paper exercise unless plans are put into effect and their results monitored. We now look at how an effective planning process controls the activities and output of an organisation. This is an essential tool for achieving optimum performance and results. The control loop consists of four distinct stages (see figure 1.4) and is a way of illustrating the planning process as a cycle of continuous change and improvement.

THE CONTROL LOOP

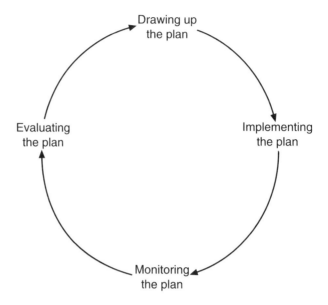

FIGURE 1.4: *The control loop.*

The essence of 'control' is looking at what has happened in practice and comparing this with what ought to have happened. This is the area of management that takes us into the concepts of **performance monitoring** and **measuring results;** it requires the use of statistics. It also takes us into **'evaluation'** (i.e. a consideration of the extent to which the plan was successful) and moves us back into planning again as new needs emerge and new developments have to be considered.

MONITORING THE PLAN

Effective planning cannot exist without the control which enables progress to be monitored.

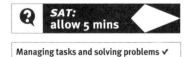

Managing tasks and solving problems ✔

ACTIVITY 7

Suggest at least two ways in which you could monitor the plan for improving health and appearance given in the commentary for activity 6.

Commentary...

You may have suggested these ways of monitoring the plan:

- taking regular measurements of waistline, hips, etc.

- weighing yourself regularly

- taking note of your fitness – can you now run for a bus or climb stairs without feeling puffed out?

- noticing that your clothes seem to fit better, or that you can indeed wear a smaller size.

Monitoring is the process of keeping a continuous check and a record of how an organisation, department or individual is progressing towards agreed objectives. It is important for several reasons:

- It may highlight weaknesses and wastage early on, so that these can be dealt with quickly and appropriately.

- It provides important information which may be used later to evaluate the success of the plan.

- Information collected during this stage can point to long-term trends and staff or departmental development needs.

Among the more important monitoring approaches that managers use are:

- regular reports based on statistical data

- special reports which are based on statistical and other data

- personal observation.

Modern computerised management information systems (MIS) can provide monthly, weekly or even daily routine information to assist managers in monitoring performance. The production manager of a bottle-filling plant, for example, would require continuous information about the number of units made, the number of rejects, labour productivity, stock and work-in-progress. As information for operational monitoring is required at frequent intervals, it is normally provided in the form of standard reports. Information for monitoring strategic plans, however, would be required on a less frequent basis.

Statistical data is best understood when:

- it is presented in the form of a chart or graph – in this way trends and relationships are much easier to identify

- it compares actual performance with projected performance – data is more meaningful if it allows managers to make this comparison

- it shows trends – extrapolating allows managers to see what will happen if the situation remains unchanged and identify whether there is a need for remedial action.

Histograms, line graphs and scatter charts are common methods for displaying statistical information graphically.

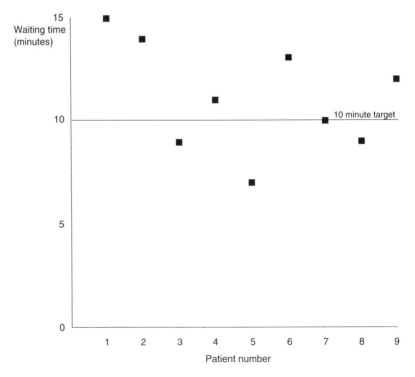

FIGURE 1.5: *Scatter diagram.*

Figure 1.5 shows a scatter diagram and is an example taken from the health service. The length of time that each outpatient waited is plotted against his or her position in the queue. The target waiting time of 10 minutes is also shown. The scatter diagram would enable managers to monitor the department's success in achieving the target waiting time.

In the next example, a line graph is used to plot actual sales against projected sales.

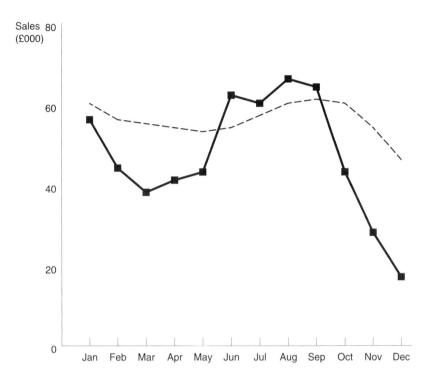

FIGURE 1.6: *Line graph.*

Figure 1.6 shows a line graph of the actual value of sales achieved throughout a 12-month period by a firm of travel agents (in solid black). The dotted line represents projected sales.

Computerised databases make it possible to produce special reports for the purpose of monitoring or control on almost any area of the organisation. Table 1.1 gives examples of the types of non-routine reports that can be produced to monitor the performance of the various business functions. Non-routine reports highlight the unusual and, in doing so, can reveal areas where significant improvements in efficiency may be achieved.

Function	Information produced to monitor performance
Accounts	Reports showing expenditure on certain items Figures showing sales linked to a special promotion
Human Resources	Figures for staff absenteeism and turnover Reasons for resigning
Marketing	Customer feedback on new products or services Customer complaints in relation to a particular product
Production	Figures for wastage Production figures for particular periods
Distribution	Numbers of customer complaints in certain geographical areas Reports on vehicle maintenance problems

TABLE 1.1: *Examples of non-routine reports used to monitor business performance*

Effective managers do not rely solely on reports and graphs to tell them what is happening in their area of operations. They recognise that monitoring by personal observation and talking to employees is also a vital source of information. A leisurely walk through the shop floor, a chat at coffee time with a group of office workers or regular visits to outlying sites can provide them with a wealth of 'qualitative' information that could not be gained in any other way. This approach to monitoring and information gathering is sometimes called 'management by wandering about' (MBWA).

> **Getting out and about is a dandy idea. But it is more than that. It is an attitude towards managing and leading. It is a way of life. It is virtually a theory of organisation unto itself. That is, it ... deals with gathering the information necessary for decision making, with making the vision concrete, with engendering commitment and risk taking, with caring about people beset with an unprecedented disruption of normal routines.**
>
> Tom Peters, 1988, *Thriving on Chaos*, Macmillan

There are many ways of monitoring plans. The important points to bear in mind are that:

- monitoring must be carried out as a systematic, continuous activity

- it is useful for managers to back up the evidence of their own eyes and ears with objective information, which can be gained by examining statistics or asking for the opinion of a third party

- recording the results of monitoring helps managers to spot trends; they can also refer to these records when they are reviewing the performance of their staff or that of the department as a whole.

Once managers have used this accumulated data to compare actual performance against the planned performance, the next stage is to decide if corrective action is needed. In effect, they must always choose between three possible courses of action:

- to continue unchanged

- to correct the performance in some way

- to revise the plan.

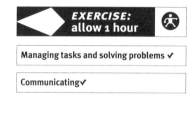

Managing tasks and solving problems ✓

Communicating ✓

ACTIVITY 8

You are team leader in the maintenance section of a plant engineering department in a large factory. This year, one of your team's objectives is to reduce overtime for preventative maintenance inspections by 60 person hours in twelve months.

You plan to achieve this objective by installing a computer system for monitoring ten machines. You are keeping track of results by analysing the monthly reports that show the overtime hours worked by the team on preventative maintenance.

Under what circumstances would you:

- continue without changing the plan?

- correct the performance?

- revise the plan?

Commentary...

You may decide to continue unchanged if:

- overtime hours are reducing in line with the target

- the general trend is in the right direction

- unexpected or unusual factors have led to a poor showing during the period under review – for example, results may have been badly affected by 'teething troubles' with the computer monitoring.

You may decide to correct the performance in some way if:

- overtime hours continue at the same rate or increase despite the introduction of the computerised system

- overtime hours decrease but there has been a low volume of machine use compared to forecast activity levels.

You may decide to revise the plan if:

- there are changes in the business 'environment' – for example, the company may have increased capacity by purchasing new machines or existing machines may be operating for longer hours due to growth in demand

- team members want to push themselves harder

- the original target was too high.

EVALUATING THE PLAN

Evaluation is the part of the planning process in which the organisation gathers evidence about how effective its plans and strategies have actually been in practice. When used as part of a continuous improvement process, it provides a basis for making decisions and allocating resources in the future.

Evaluation is the final stage of the control loop introduced earlier, but because the planning cycle is a continuous process, it is also the starting point for the next round of planning.

Evaluation centres around four procedures:

1. establishing criteria which can be used as measures of success

2. identifying the information needed to assess how far these criteria have been met

3. collecting information or data

4. analysing and interpreting the data.

Because an evaluation should concern itself not only with the achievement of goals and objectives but also with the process by which they are achieved the criteria which managers should consider fall into two main categories:

1. the outcomes of the plan

2. the way the outcomes are achieved.

The **outcomes of the plan** include:

- the achievement of goals and objectives

- benefits which were unplanned or unexpected.

The actual criteria selected under this heading will depend on the goals and objectives that are identified in the first place. For example, if the objective is 'to improve our customer satisfaction rating by 5 per cent', the criterion for evaluation will be 'customer satisfaction'. If the objective is 'to reduce waste by 50 per cent', the criterion will be 'waste reduction', and so on.

When considering the **way the outcomes are achieved,** you might look at:

- the appropriateness of the strategies selected

- the quality and sufficiency of the resources used.

Here, managers could use the same evaluation criteria used to select the strategies when the plan was being drawn up. Managers could ask the following questions:

- Were the strategies **suitable?** (Did they exploit our strengths? Did they fit in with our purposes?)

- Were the strategies **feasible?** (Were there enough resources? Did we cope well with competitive reactions?)

- Were the strategies **acceptable?** (Did they result in an increase in profit? How did stakeholders react to the structural and cultural changes?)

The nature of the evaluation criteria determines what information needs to be gathered. If they are carrying out regular monitoring, managers are already collecting information which they can use to evaluate the plan. The important point is to use this same evidence to define not only whether or not the objectives have been achieved but also the extent to which the plan itself is valid and appropriate.

Managers may wish to supplement quantitative information (which can measured and presented statistically and numerically) with qualitative information (e.g. how stakeholders feel about particular strategies). A common way of collecting qualitative information is to conduct a survey of customers', shareholders' or employees' opinions using questionnaires or interviews. For a thorough evaluation, it is usually best to use a mixture of both methods.

Evaluation provides information that be used to develop new plans, to review existing activities and to improve or eliminate ineffective or inappropriate strategies. But this will not happen unless the information that has been collected is not only collated, but also analysed and interpreted appropriately. When examining the data, managers need to ask the following questions:

- What does this information tell us about the validity and effectiveness of our objectives and plans?

- What changes do we now need to make to our strategies and activities?

- What further needs can we identify as a result of the evaluation?

- Are our conclusions and recommendations supported by data?

Ideally, the findings of the evaluation should be presented in a verbal or written report, supported by appropriate data in the form of tables, graphs and diagrams. In this way, evaluation can be used to change and improve the practice of planning throughout the organisation.

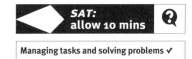

SAT:
allow 10 mins

Managing tasks and solving problems ✓

ACTIVITY 9

Use these statements to test your understanding of the key facts about evaluation. Say whether each one is true or false and, if false, explain why.

(a) Evaluation provides evidence of the effectiveness of the people employed by the organisation.

(b) Evaluation is the final stage of the planning cycle.

(c) The first stage of evaluation is to establish criteria which can be used to measure the success of the plan.

(d) Evaluation should only be concerned with whether the plan was successful in meeting its goals and objectives.

(e) The three criteria for evaluating strategies are suitability, feasibility, and measurability.

(f) Quantitative information will tell managers how people reacted to the strategies selected in the plan.

(g) It is pointless doing an evaluation unless this leads to change and improvement.

Commentary...

Statement (a) is false. Evaluation provides evidence of the effectiveness of the organisation's plans and strategies.

Statement (b) is true, but evaluation is also the starting point for the next round of planning.

Statement (c) is true.

Statement (d) is false. Evaluation should concern itself not only with the achievement of goals and objectives but also with the process (or strategies) by which they were achieved.

Statement (e) is false. The three criteria for evaluating strategies are suitability, feasibility, and acceptability.

Statement (f) is false. Qualitative information will tell managers how people reacted to the strategies selected in the plan.

Statement (h) is true.

summary

▶ Planning helps everyone in the organisation to know its goals and objectives and how they are expected to achieve them. It bridges the gap from where the organisation is now to where it wants to be.

▶ The main types of plans examined in this workbook are long-term strategic plans, shorter-term operational plans and contingency plans which can be attached to any sort of plan.

▶ In some organisations, the manager is expected to set objectives for his or her staff, the overall process is very much a top-down one. Some other organisations encourage employees at all levels to participate in objective setting.

▶ Most types of plans have a number of elements in common: goals, objectives, strategies, tactics or tasks.

▶ An effective planning process incorporates a 'cascade' system in which overall goals created at the top of an organisation flow down through the levels so that departments, teams and individuals know how they can contribute to achieving them.

▶ The control loop is a cycle of continuous change and improvement, consisting of four distinct stages: drawing up the plan, implementing the plan, monitoring the plan, and evaluating the plan.

Types of plan

STRATEGIC PLANS

OPERATIONAL PLANS

BUDGETS

PROJECT PLANS

Objectives

After participating in this session, you should be able to:

▶ distinguish between operational and strategic plans

▶ evaluate the objectives of the marketing function within the overall organisational plan

▶ describe a range of plans that are commonly used in organisations

▶ draw up a project plan.

In working through this session, you will practise the following BTEC common skills:

Managing and developing self	✔
Working with and relating to others	✔
Communicating	✔
Managing tasks and solving problems	✔
Applying numeracy	
Applying technology	✔
Applying design and creativity	

Strategic plans

In their book *Exploring Corporate Strategy,* Johnson and Scholes (Prentice Hall, 1993) identify six characteristics of strategic decisions and plans.

1. Strategic decisions are likely to be concerned with the scope of an organisation's activities. Does (and should) the organisation concentrate on one activity, or does it have many? The issue of scope is fundamental to strategic plans because it concerns the way in which those responsible for managing the organisation perceive its boundaries. It is to do with what they want the organisation to be about.

2. Strategy is to do with the matching of the activities of an organisation to the **environment** within which it operates. In particular, it needs to take into account political pressures, economic conditions, social trends and technological advances. We discuss these environmental influences in greater detail in session 4 of this section of the workbook.

3. Strategic planning is about matching the organisation's activities to its **resource capability**. There would be little point in attempting to take advantage of a new business opportunity if the resources required are not available and could not be made available. Strategic decisions often have major resource implications for an organisation.

4. Strategic decisions are likely to **affect operational decisions,** setting off waves of 'lesser decisions'. We shall see later in the session how the various business functions derive their own plans from the strategic plans for the company as a whole.

5. Strategic plans, once their implementation is under way, can be **difficult to change**. The resource and material demands of strategic plans frequently require a long-term commitment that is hard to reverse.

6. Strategic plans are affected by the values and expectations of those who have power in and around the organisation. Strategic plans usually reflect the attitudes and beliefs of those who have most influence on an organisation – its **stakeholders**.

The stakeholders of a public or private sector business organisation are those people and groups who have a 'stake' in its success; they have some reason for wanting it to achieve certain objectives. As we shall see later, stakeholders often have conflicting requirements or expectations, and this factor can cause problems when businesses are trying to set their strategic objectives. Stakeholders can be:

- **internal** – usually people or groups who work within the organisation, e.g. employees and managers

- **external** – people or groups who are connected with the organisation in some way, but are outside it, e.g. suppliers, customers and shareholders.

ACTIVITY 1

Make two lists to identify the main internal and external stakeholders of a typical limited company.

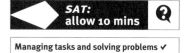

SAT: allow 10 mins

Managing tasks and solving problems ✔

Commentary...

Internal stakeholders are, for example:

- the Board of Directors
- the management team
- work teams
- project teams
- departments or functions
- individual managers and employees
- the staff association or trades unions
- sports and leisure teams.

External stakeholders may be:

- shareholders
- organisations and individuals who supply goods and services
- individual customers
- consumer organisations
- the community at large
- taxpayers
- local and national government.

Johnson and Scholes provide a useful definition of a strategic plan:

Strategy is the direction and scope of an organisation over the long term: ideally which matches its resources to its changing environment and, in particular, its markets, customers and clients so as to meet stakeholder expectations.

Johnson, G. and Scholes, G., 1993, *Exploring Corporate Strategy*, Prentice Hall

What distinguishes strategic plans from other types of management plans is that they are often of a higher order of complexity; they involve a considerable degree of uncertainty and they demand an integrated approach to managing the organisation.

Managers frequently have to cross functional boundaries to deal with strategic problems and to come to agreements with other managers who may have different interests and different priorities. One way of achieving this is to form cross-functional management teams whose aim is to improve communications, increase understanding of each other's priorities and to solve problems.

IDENTIFYING PRIORITIES FOR STRATEGIC PLANS

We have seen that plans are vital to business success and that, to be effective, those plans must incorporate a number of different elements. But how can planners arrive at the right objectives? How can they ensure that they have included the correct balance of priorities?

It is important to note that although the profit objective is clearly of importance, by itself, it is not sufficient for the effective management of a business organisation. There are many other considerations and motivations which affect the overall goal of making the greatest profit or achieving maximum economic efficiency.

In his book, *The Practice of Management* (first published by Heinemann in the mid-1950s, reprinted in paperback in 1994), Peter Drucker suggests the eight key areas in which objectives should be set at a corporate level.

1. **Market standing:** e.g. increasing market share, developing the product range and improving customer loyalty and satisfaction.

2. **Innovation:** e.g. harnessing developments arising from technological advancements and introducing new processes or improvements in all major areas of organisational activity.

3. **Productivity:** e.g. making optimum use of resources and introducing innovative techniques and systems to increase output and quality.

4. **Physical and financial resources:** e.g. effective management of plant, machinery, offices, factory space, budgeting and ensuring the supply of capital.

5. **Profitability:** e.g. maximising profit and using yardsticks for measuring profitability.

6. **Manager performance and development:** e.g. developing future managers, removing layers of management, guiding and supporting managers.

7. **Worker performance and attitude:** e.g. improving employee relations, developing team work, encouraging employee involvement.

8. **Public responsibility:** e.g. fulfilling responsibilities towards society and the public interest, meeting legal demands and responding to public opinion.

To emphasise only profit misdirects managers to the point where they may endanger the survival of the business. To obtain profit today, they tend to undermine the future. They may push the most easily saleable product lines and slight those that are the market of tomorrow. They tend to short-change research, promotion and other postponable investments. Above all, they shy away from any capital expenditure that may increase the invested capital base against which profits are measured; and the result is the dangerous obsolescence of equipment.

Peter Drucker, 1994, *The Practice of Management,* Butterworth Heinemann

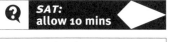

SAT:
allow 10 mins

Managing tasks and solving problems ✓

ACTIVITY 2

Into which of Drucker's eight key areas do the following objectives fit?

During this financial year we will:

(a) reduce the sales process cycle time by 5 per cent

(b) increase customer satisfaction by 3 per cent

(c) devolve day-to-day running of the unit to teams and their leaders

(d) reduce waste by 10 per cent

(e) allow team analysis of performance and identification of improvement opportunities.

Commentary...

You should have noted that objective

    (a) relates to productivity

    (b) relates to market standing

    (c) relates to worker performance and attitude

    (d) relates to profitability

    (e) relates to worker performance and attitude.

STAKEHOLDER EXPECTATIONS

When setting and prioritising strategic goals and objectives, managers ignore at their peril the views and expectations of the organisation's stakeholders. As we have seen, stakeholders are groups or individuals who have a stake in, or an expectation of, an organisation's performance. Although individuals rarely have sufficient power to determine unilaterally the objectives or strategy of an organisation, they can be influential when they form part of a stakeholder group.

The water industry has provided some excellent examples of companies which have failed to maintain their awareness of stakeholder expectations. It seems that since privatisation, many of them have failed to maintain a balance of objectives and have ignored the expectations of a large and vociferous stakeholder group – the people in the community at large who use their services on a daily basis.

By overlooking the requirements of this group, the water companies have attracted so much hostility – particularly during the 1995 drought – that it will probably take them years to recover the lost ground.

IT NEVER RAINS

Although they talk constantly about the weather, the British are curiously unprepared for it. Thus, without fail, as the first autumn leaves tumble on to the tracks, the railways grind to a halt. And when, as now, it fails to rain for several months during summer, the water companies run short of water. Hosepipe bans now apply in parts of the country and, on August 9th 1995, Yorkshire Water asked the Department of the Environment for permission to make 'drought orders', which might mean cutting off supplies to up to 600,000 customers, making them use standpipes. Customers thought that privatisation, which took place in December 1989, was supposed to bring an end to such problems, particularly as water charges have risen sharply in real terms since then. It did not; and the Labour Party has tapped their consequent irritation, pointing out that while customers are going short, up to 30 per cent of the water produced by the industry leaks away before it reaches the customer.

This is far from fair. Since privatisation, the industry has invested £15 billion in new infrastructure (indeed, financing such investment was privatisation's purpose). Not all of this has been directed at boosting supply – most has gone to improve water quality and sewage disposal – but leakages are down. Thames Water's new £250m ring main means that hosepipe bans may be history for London. Still, it is not obvious that water companies should seek to provide unlimited amounts of water in all circumstances. Yorkshire Water aims to meet demand in 49 years out of 50: this year's minimal rainfall in parts of Yorkshire is likely to be exceeded in 91 years out of 92.

Life is going to get tougher still for the water companies. In July, the Monopolies and Mergers Commission responded to an appeal by South-west Water against a much tougher price cap imposed last year by the regulator, Ofwat, by imposing an even tougher cap. When Ofwat reviews the cap again, in 2000, it seems certain to hit the companies even harder. And before then, a Labour government may be elected, promising a windfall tax on utility profits and a new price cap which automatically splits unexpectedly large profits between shareholders and customers.

To widespread amazement, six of the ten privatised water companies recently awarded rebates to their customers – worth between £6 and £40 per household – to allow them to share in the benefits of private ownership. This fit of generosity may have been brought on by Labour's threat, and by the companies' unpopularity.

Source: *The Economist,* August 12th 1995, p.25

**SAT:
allow 15 mins**

Managing tasks and solving problems ✔

ACTIVITY 3

Read the case study above about the water industry. Describe why the water industry's customers have been particularly irritated about hosepipe bans and drought orders.

Explain how a future Labour government proposes to manage the conflict between shareholders' and customers' interests. Note what some water companies are doing to alleviate their customers' hostility.

Commentary...

You should have noted that customers have been irritated about hosepipe bans and drought orders because they thought that privatisation would put an end to such problems.

A future Labour government proposes to manage the conflict between shareholders' and customers' interests by imposing a windfall tax on utility profits and dividing unexpectedly large profits between shareholders and customers.

Some water companies are alleviating their customers' hostility by awarding rebates of between £6 and £40 per household.

Most individuals belong to more than one stakeholder group. For example, it is possible for a employee to be both a shareholder and a user of a company's services. What emerges is the need to identify different stakeholder groups, to understand their expectations and to weigh these in terms of the power that they exercise.

As the expectations of different groups are often likely to differ, it is normal for conflict to exist regarding the importance or desirability of different objectives. In most situations, organisations have to make a compromise between expectations which cannot all be achieved simultaneously – between, for example, growth and profitability, cost efficiency and jobs, and control and independence.

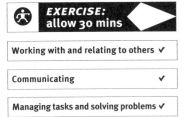

EXERCISE:
allow 30 mins

Working with and relating to others ✔

Communicating ✔

Managing tasks and solving problems ✔

ACTIVITY 4

Working in small groups, first identify some of the external and internal stakeholder groups of your college.

Having agreed on the stakeholders, describe what their expectations or requirements might be. Identify areas where the expectations of your college's stakeholders may be in conflict.

Use the box below to summarise the findings of your group.

Commentary...

You may have identified the following stakeholders and expectations.

External stakeholders	Expectations
Students' union	That students should have the opportunity to participate in union activities, organise themselves and develop their political understanding
Lecturers' unions	That teaching staff should receive appropriate terms and conditions, maintain their professional standing and work in an environment that is both safe and healthy
Parents	That the college should continually improve its results and its position in the 'league table'; good pastoral care and a broad curriculum
Government	That the college will produce required outcomes and value for money
Local and national industry	That the college will train students in the skills required by local and national companies
Local community	That the college will make a contribution to the life of the community

Internal stakeholders	Expectations
Students	That the college will help them to achieve their personal and vocational aims and objectives
Lecturers	That the college will support and help them to fulfil their professional responsibilities
Departments	That the college will provide them with the resources necessary to fulfil their objectives
College principal	That the college will achieve his/her vision of academic excellence and service
Senior managers/heads of schools	That the college will provide them with the resources necessary to support staff and students

You might have noted that there may be conflicts in the following areas:

- between the government's expectation of cost efficiency and the college's need for better resources

- between parents' expectation of pastoral care and examination board's requirement for high quality educational provision

- between lecturers' unions' expectation for good terms and conditions and the college's need to spend money on areas other than staff salaries

- between students' union expectation that students be allowed to become involved in student politics and the time imposed by the lecturers requirements.

In their book, *Exploring Corporate Strategy,* Johnson and Scholes (Prentice Hall, 1993) provide some useful examples of common conflicts of expectations. Here are a few of the examples that they provide:

- There may be a conflict between the requirement for short-term profitability and the need to invest money so that the business can grow.

- In small businesses, there may be conflicts between owners' and managers' ideas.

- A company's financial interests and the interests of employees may conflict – cost efficiency through capital investment can sometimes mean job losses.

- In public services, a common conflict is between mass provision and specialist services.

- In public services, savings in one area, e.g. social security benefits, may result in increases elsewhere, e.g. school meals or medical care.

Effective planning requires organisations to map various stakeholders' expectations and to understand where they might conflict. This exercise helps them to decide:

- what objectives are necessary and appropriate

- how easy or difficult various courses of action are likely to be

- how such conflicts can be managed.

Businesses frequently try to draw together the expectations of different groups and individuals by means of mission **statements** or policies. These allow everyone involved to have their viewpoint taken into consideration before strategic plans are made. We explore this approach in session 3.

ACTIVITY 5

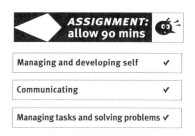

ASSIGNMENT:
allow 90 mins

Managing and developing self	✓
Communicating	✓
Managing tasks and solving problems	✓

Write a report (of approximately 1500 words) on stakeholder expectations at your college or business and how they affect planning priorities. Point out any areas where these priorities might conflict and how such conflicts are (or might be) managed.

You may like to use the following headings in your report.

- ◉ A definition of stakeholders

- ◉ The expectations of internal stakeholders

- ◉ The expectations of external stakeholders

- ◉ How college plans have been influenced by stakeholder expectations

- ◉ Areas of conflict or potential conflict

- ◉ How the college has managed (or could manage) such conflicts

Use separate sheets of paper to write your report and note the main points of your answer in the box below.

Operational plans

This type of plan is concerned with how the different functions of the organisation – marketing, personnel, production and so on – contribute to its strategic plan. For example, a company that wishes to establish as a strategic objective that it intends to sell 20 per cent of its product in the export market would need to break this down into operational plans for the different functions:

- The sales department has to set detailed targets for overseas orders, and to set up systems for dealing with these.

- The production manager must identify design changes imposed by the international specification.

- The finance department has to establish systems for currency exchange and international credit.

- The training department has to set objectives to do with developing language skills, export marketing procedures and awareness of different cultures.

There will be other objectives and targets in different parts of the organisation: distribution, research and development, customer services and other functions will each play a part in the overall strategy.

So, operational objectives have to be aligned with those of the organisation and operational plans should produce a blueprint which managers and teams can follow to achieve the agreed objectives. An effective operational plan states who is going to do what, by when, with what resources and to what standard. It should be a simple means of communicating and avoiding confusion.

In *Making Management Decisions (2nd edn)*, Steve Cook and Nigel Slack (Prentice Hall, 1991) set out a framework of operational performance, and argue that objectives specified in operational plans tend to fit into the following categories:

- **Technical specification:** improving products and services, bringing them closer to what customers want

- **Quality:** reducing errors, getting things right first time

- **Responsiveness:** shortening the time customers have to wait for their goods and services

- **Dependability:** increasing the chances of things happening when they are supposed to happen

- **Flexibility:** increasing the flexibility of the operation – in terms of the range of things that can be done or the speed of doing them

Human factors are central to how any operational plan, no matter how good it looks on paper, is implemented. Making the plan realistic, workable and relevant requires keeping one eye on the objectives and the other on people and their behaviour.

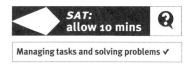

SAT:
allow 10 mins

Managing tasks and solving problems ✔

ACTIVITY 6

Read the following statements. Which relate to operational plans and which to strategic plans?

(a) These plans affect the long-term direction of an organisation.

(b) These plans identify how the different functions will contribute to the overall goals of the organisation.

(c) These plans are to do with the scope of an organisation's activities.

(d) These plans are a way of communicating directly to teams and individuals how they can contribute to the success of the organisation.

(e) Business success usually depends on decisions that are taken at this level.

Commentary...

Statements (a) and (c) relate to strategic plans. Statements (b) and (d) relate to operational plans. Statement (e) relates to both strategic and operational plans.

Rosabeth Moss Kanter put forward a clear picture of how organisations need to integrate the plans of their various functions and departments if they are going to cope effectively in today's business environment. She talks of 'integrative systems' where, among other strengths:

- people within and between departments work together

- everyone sees problems as common problems and not just as a difficulty for some other department

- teams are valued

- the culture and structure encourage everyone to view these functions in an integrated way.

Such organisations reduce rancorous conflict and isolation between organisational units; create mechanisms for exchange of information and new ideas across organisational boundaries; ensure that multiple perspectives will be taken into account in decisions; and provide coherence and direction to the whole organisation.

Rosabeth Moss Kanter, 1985, *The Change Masters,* Allen & Unwin

A number of related strategies can be used to achieve integrative systems:

- breaking down the barriers between departments and functions by networking and teamworking

- breaking down the barriers between managers and subordinates by encouraging them to create good relationships

- establishing an organisational 'climate' of openness and mutual trust

- recognising and rewarding individuals and groups who have performed well.

MARKETING PLANS

The marketing plan is one of the most important of an organisation's operational plans. The following case study examines the process of marketing planning and gives an insight into the nature of operational plans and how they are derived from strategic plans. You can read more about marketing planning in *Market Relations*, a companion volume in this series.

SOURIRE COSMETICS

Sourire is in the market for both cosmetics and toiletries. Sourire has a strategic objective to achieve a 20 per cent increase in profits during the next five years.

The company has decided to withdraw its cosmetic toothpaste (Smile) because of adverse publicity from dentists. Two other products are to be phased out: medicated facial wipes (Dermaclear Pads) and breath freshener (Fragrispray). Its long-term strategy includes a plan to produce a number of new products in each market including three types of skincare products (enriched with vitamins and minerals) in the cosmetics market and two ranges of soaps and shampoos (also with vitamins and minerals) in the toiletries market.

This strategy will require a financial investment in research and production, the recruitment and training of new staff and the drawing up of an appropriate marketing plan. Like any other plan, the marketing plan will include objectives based on the company's strategic objectives and a set of strategies designed to achieve those objectives.

So, Sourire's corporate objectives might include:

- **target sales** for each product over a specified period of time – to achieve sales of 200,000 bottles of skin cleanser, 100,000 bottles of skin toner and 60,000 bottles of eye lotion over three years
- a **market share** figure for each product – e.g. to achieve a market share of 15 per cent of the skincare market within five years
- **profit objectives** for each product – £500,000 profit on all skincare products each year for the next three years.

Sourire's marketing strategies indicate how these sales, market share and profit figures will be achieved. The marketing department decides to use a number of integrated marketing strategies, based on the 'market position' that has been identified for these products. (They are positioned as chic, high-price products; the target market is health- and style-conscious professional women.) The strategies involve market research, advertising, promotion and packaging.

ACTIVITY 7

Read this slightly fuller list of objectives and strategies identified by Sourire's marketing department.

Objectives, to achieve:

- sales of 200,000 bottles of skin cleanser, 100,000 bottles of skin toner and 60,000 bottles of eye lotion over three years

- sales of 250,000 soaps and 300,000 bottles of shampoo in one year

- a 5 per cent share of the skincare market, 8 per cent of the

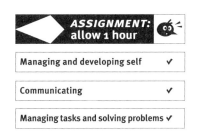

ASSIGNMENT: allow 1 hour

Managing and developing self	✔
Communicating	✔
Managing tasks and solving problems	✔

market for soaps and shampoos and 10 per cent of the cosmetic toothpaste market within five years

- £500,000 profit on all skincare products each year for the next three years

- £150,000 profit on both Dermaclear and Fragrispray during the next year.

Strategies:

- **market research** – to find out how best to present, promote and sell the new products

- **advertising** – a media campaign mainly in magazines that are read by working women; Dermaclear and Fragrispray will be advertised in publications aimed at teenage girls

- **promotion** – a month-by-month plan to increase consumers' awareness

- **packaging** – existing products to be re-packaged to catch the eye and to underline the market position of the products.

Discuss whether these objectives and strategies are correctly based on long-term corporate objectives. Which ones might be inappropriate, and why?

Prepare an outline marketing plan on one side of A4 incorporating a realistic set of marketing objectives correctly derived from the company's corporate objectives.

Summarise the main points of your answer in the box below.

PLANS FOR INDIVIDUALS

Operational plans are frequently translated into action plans or personal development plans for individuals. These plans frequently, but by no means always, form part of a performance appraisal system, in which managers ensure that individual targets and achievements support the organisation's strategic and operational goals.

Michelin, for example, has produced an appraisal scheme at its UK sites. All staff undergo an annual performance and development review with their line manager and the appraisal is countersigned by the next level of management and used as the basis for planning training.

However, as Bob Garratt argues, appraisal schemes are often far from perfect:

> **Most appraisal schemes are damned by those who use and suffer them as worse than useless. Rather than measure, debate and plan individual development and work targets ... they become either an organisational joke or a way for managers to assert control over their staff.**

> Bob Garratt, 1994, *Creating a Learning Organisation, 2nd edn,* Harper Collins

Garratt contends that effective appraisal schemes should:

- be an exchange of ideas between manager and team member in which present performance, future possibilities and targets are discussed – not a one-sided telling off

- relate to measurable work performance and target setting

- focus on observable behaviours, rather than speculate on fuzzy guesses of personal qualities

- draw out training and development needs and contain a commitment to take action on these

- identify possible career steps and goals

- incorporate a fair appeal system.

Some schemes are also linked to pay and rewards structures. While Garratt favours such an approach, many other people feel this can be counter-productive and places too great a burden on the scheme.

Budgets

Budgets are often described as 'the economic expressions of operational or strategic plans'. One of the major advantages of budgeting is that it demands a structured approach and, because a budget is in the form of numbers, it forces precision in planning. A budget can be seen as a map or a chart, helping you to reach where you want to go.

A budget defines how an organisation intends to allocate its financial resources to achieve agreed objectives. This resource allocation is expressed in monthly or yearly totals for each function or department within the organisation. A budget enables assumptions about the future to be examined, discussed, tested and adjusted.

Two main categories of expenditure are reflected in financial plans and statements:

1. **Revenue budgets** allocate money for day-to-day running costs, e.g. salaries, supplies, heating, lighting, raw materials and other consumables.

2. **Capital budgets** identify expenditure incurred on acquiring or reproducing fixed assets, or on improving or extending them.

Fixed assets are those assets acquired by a business for retention beyond the current accounting period and not held for the purpose of resale. Revenue expenditure, on the other hand is fully consumed within the period in which it is acquired.

BUDGET SETTING

Most organisations use one of two budget setting processes: incremental budgeting and zero-based budgeting (see *Managing Finance and Information*, a companion volume in this series).

Incremental budgeting (also called historic-based budgeting) works on the assumption that the budget for the next financial year will be the same as the budget for this year, but with minor adjustments to allow for price increases, pay awards and any changes in services or processes. This approach to budget setting is most often used because it is easy for managers who are not financial experts to understand. Some of its disadvantages are that:

- future expenditure may be difficult to predict

- it is geared to preserving the status quo and costs can be perpetuated simply because they have always been in the budget

- the real pattern of expenditure may be distorted by moving resources from one budget heading to another (this is called **virement**) and, if this is done for several years, the budget can become meaningless.

Zero-based budgeting is a costly and time-consuming alternative and, as such, is less common. However, it can be useful for overhauling and improving the financial plan. Zero-based budgeting assumes that the budget has never been set before and requires managers to decide what they want to do, how much this will cost and to justify the desired level of expenditure.

Budgets are not always fixed amounts handed down from a higher management level; they are most valuable if they are used as a tool for negotiating priorities and for devolving accountability to operational managers for the performance of their departments or teams.

However, making managers responsible for their expenditure means that they have to be involved in agreeing the overall expenditure and how much can be allocated to different areas of work. Effective budgeting is usually a 'top and bottom' exercise, in which functions, departments or teams have the opportunity to propose and bargain with the management tier which has the power to allocate funds.

The objective of these discussions is to reduce costs, while maintaining or increasing efficiency. Setting a budget is an ideal opportunity for managers to consider the following questions:

- What scope is there for altering and improving working methods?

- Does this budget adequately reflect and integrate with our operational plans for the coming year?

- Is it possible to seek savings in lower priority areas to 'trade off' for extra spending on higher priority or higher benefit activities?

So, the budget setting is most frequently an iterative process, in which budget holders and top management negotiate until they can agree on the best distribution of financial resources.

Managers can achieve a number of important benefits by involving themselves more closely in the budgeting process. Because they have contributed to planning and budget decisions, they will become more responsible for ensuring, as far as they are able, that expenditure is kept within the agreed limits. The planning process helps to make goals explicit and the budget helps them to assign priorities to those goals. They can begin to think more creatively about ways of using resources more flexibly.

CONTROLLING THE BUDGET

Once a budget has been drawn up, it can be used as a control tool by comparing actual expenditure with budgeted expenditure. Individual departments or teams pass information about their expenditure back to the finance function, where this information is co-ordinated at an organisation level.

The obvious advantage of working out a budget in advance is that, with careful monitoring each month, managers can avoid getting into financial difficulties. If things do go wrong, they can use the budget to identify areas of potential saving. But budgets are much more than this. They are also dynamic tools for change that can secure more effective performance at departmental level and contribute to the success of the organisation as a whole.

If budget holders do overspending they have the following options:

- cut back spending in the areas where the overspending has occurred

- cut back in other areas and move the savings made to the heading where the overspending has occurred

- ask the finance function to provide more funds.

If the latter option is selected, the manager concerned would have to build an effective case for a budget increase, basing his or her argument on hard facts.

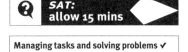

SAT:
allow 15 mins

Managing tasks and solving problems ✔

ACTIVITY 8

Summarise the uses and benefits of budgets at both organisational and department level.

Commentary...

Here are some reasons why a budget is both necessary and valuable.

○ It is a **statement of policy:** a budget explains the purposes for which various amounts of money have been allocated – the human and material resources that it is intended to purchase. The budget is a statement of the budget holder's values and policies in that it indicates the relative importance given to different areas.

○ It is a useful **tool for forecasting:** the discipline of drawing up a budget for the period ahead forces managers to forecast their future resource requirements in the light of the expected demand for their products and services.

○ It makes budget holders **accountable:** once a budget has been created, budget holders are accountable for the way that their organisations or departments perform in relation to the agreed plan.

○ It allows expenditure to be **monitored:** by carefully monitoring the money spent month by month, it is possible to identify problems early and take corrective action.

ANALYSING A BUDGET

Here is a typical budget statement for a ward manager in an NHS Trust, showing clearly the set budget, actual expenditure and variances, i.e. over or underspending.

Summary of expenditure	Current month			Year to date		
	Budget £	Actual £	Variance £	Budget £	Actual £	Variance £
Nursing staff	14,309	13,940	-369	42,927	40,219	-2,708
Allocated expenses	4,964	5,283	319	15,049	16,154	1,105
Direct budget allocation	19,273	19,223	-50	57,976	56,373	-1,603
Apportioned overheads	9,696	11,507	1,811	29,346	32,066	2,720
Total expenditure	**28,969**	**30,730**	**1,761**	**87,322**	**88,439**	**1,117**

If you are not familiar with this type of statement you may find the following definitions helpful. **Allocated expenses** are largely consumables (e.g. bandages, drugs, syringes, stationery) and services (e.g. X-ray or physiotherapy) which the ward requires and obtains from other departments. **Apportioned overheads** are the share of the cost of overheads (e.g. heating, maintenance or grass mowing) which are attributable to particular budget holders. For instance, heating might be apportioned to departments on the basis of square footage of space occupied.

It is important for managers to check that budget statements are accurate and that expenditure is listed under the correct headings.

EXERCISE: allow 30 mins

Communicating	✓
Managing tasks and solving problems	✓

ACTIVITY 9

This activity helps you to become more familiar with this type of budget statement. With a partner, study this budget report and start to analyse it by deciding whether you think the following statements are true or false. If you think they are false, explain why.

(a) Nearly three quarters of direct budget costs for this ward arise from nurse staffing.

(b) The total budget for the whole year is £57,976.

(c) This month, and during the year to date, the ward has overspent on consumables.

(d) This month the ward has spent too much on nursing staff.

(e) The ward has overspent on its budget both for the current month and the year to date.

Commentary...

(a) True: staff costs throughout the NHS account for 70–80 per cent of total expenditure.

(b) False: the total budget for the whole year is not given – for the year to date it is £87,322.

(c) True: this is an area which the ward manager will have to examine to find out how the overspending has arisen.

(d) False: the ward has underspent on nursing staff.

(e) True: the situation is not yet serious, but could become so unless the ward manager takes decisive action.

The NHS Trust budget statement is only a summary, and further reports would show the detail of expenditure on staffing, consumables, services and overheads. By analysing this breakdown of actual costs, a manager can identify areas where changes have to be introduced and costs must be cut, so that the budget can be adhered to more closely.

BUSINESS PLANS

The term 'business plan' is most frequently used in the context of small businesses. Banks frequently ask to see a business plan before they will agree to make a loan to an organisation. But you also come across the term in larger organisations where responsibility for operational budgets has been devolved to individual units or departments. In this situation, a manager drawing up a business plan is making a case for the resources that he or she needs to achieve identified goals or targets.

Whether it is seeking internal approval or external finance, the focus of the plan will be on:

- setting realistic goals and performance targets

- demonstrating how these will be met

- identifying the resources required to achieve the plan.

If the plan is written for consideration by a bank manager or venture capitalist, the business plan may also contain details of:

- the background of the business

- its main products or services

- facts about the industry or sector that the business operates in, the market, the competition and proposed marketing activities

- information about the business' production or service operation processes

- a description of the way in which the business is organised and managed

- a financial analysis predicting sales and profits before tax for three to five years ahead.

Project plans

Project management refers to the task of planning and controlling one-off projects. A number of characteristics distinguish projects from other management activities:

- They have a single specific purpose.

- They have a definite start and end time.

- They have a definite budget.

- They usually incorporate a number of tasks that have to be completed in fixed phases.

- The project team may comprise people from different departments, and may also include people from outside the organisation.

Managing tasks and solving problems ✓

ACTIVITY 10

In the following list, which items would you classify as projects?

(a) Attending meetings of the senior management team

(b) Designing an induction pack for new employees

(c) The purchase and introduction of a new piece of equipment

(d) Moving to new premises

(e) Allocating tasks and organising staff in a department of a large store

(f) Organising a conference

(g) Putting together a directory of voluntary organisations

(h) Managing a system of staff appraisals

Commentary...

Activities (a), (e) and (h) are not projects because they do not have a distinct start and end time, nor do they have a single purpose. The other activities meet most of the criteria identified above, and can be classed as projects.

Activity 10 gives another clue that helps us to distinguish between projects and routine management activity. Projects are usually designed to create new systems or to develop the organisation or its products in some way. A project team will only be successful if it has a clear aim, a well-defined task and the composition of the team is chosen with care.

PROJECT PLANNING

Successful projects require careful planning; a plan enables the project manager to identify the major phases of the project and the time-scales and resources that will be required at each stage. The plan will enable the team to monitor its progress during the life of the project and to identify any adjustment that may be needed if the goal is to be attained within the agreed deadline.

A typical plan might contain the following details:

- A summary of the requirements of the project

- The aims and objectives of the project

- A description of how the project will be managed, and what process will be used

- Who will be involved

- The budget, material resources and facilities that will be used

- A timetable for the project – usually called a 'project schedule'

The time-scale for a project schedule can vary considerably – from a matter of weeks to, in the case of very large projects, several years. Each schedule lists:

- the tasks

- when these are to be done

- the sequence in which they should be carried out

and, optionally, who is responsible for them.

A schedule can be prepared either manually or using a computer. A number of scheduling techniques are used in business organisations, including manually produced activity schedules, Gantt charts and the critical path method.

In his book, *The Effective Manager*, Gordon Torry (Wrightbooks, 1990) outlines the main stages in the preparation of a schedule for a small project as follows:

1. Define the objectives and the desired outputs of the project, and specify the key deadlines to be incorporated.

2. Identify the staff and other resources that need to be involved. If possible, call a meeting of those people and carry out steps 3-5 below.

3. List all the tasks needed to complete the project and place them in a logical sequence of operation. Notice groupings and links between tasks. For example, Task B cannot start before Task A is complete, but C can run parallel to either A or B.

4. Estimate how long each task should take.

5. Prepare a draft chart based on:

   - the list of tasks

   - the sequence and relationship of tasks

   - how long each task should take

- the required completion date.

6. After the meeting draw up a formal schedule which shows:

- the tasks in the order in which they are to be carried out

- when they are to be performed and how long is allowed

- who is responsible for each task.

Copies are issued to all participants with their contributions highlighted and each person reports back as they carry out their allocated tasks.

It is important to be aware of slippage, e.g. through staff sickness, and if at all possible to build in space for unexpected events. Figure 2.1 shows an example of a manually produced activity schedule for the production of an information pack for a voluntary housing organisation.

Task	Duration (days)	Starts	Ends	Person responsible
Plan contents of brochure	7	2 Jan 96	10 Jan 96	HK, RF, PT, EP
Draw up mailing list	15	11 Jan 96	31 Jan 96	EP
Write first draft	15	11 Jan 96	31 Jan 96	HK
Review first draft	7	1 Feb 96	9 Feb 96	RF, PT
Research pictures	16	12 Feb 96	4 Mar 96	PT
Edit first draft	7	12 Feb 96	20 Feb 96	HK
Send out for comment	13	21 Feb 96	8 Mar 96	EP
Collect and collate feedback	19	11 Mar 96	9 April 96	EP
Incorporate amendments	10	10 April 96	23 April 96	HK
Edit final manual script	3	24 April 96	26 Apr 96	RF
DTP	3	29 April 96	1 May 96	C
Printing	14	2 May 96	22 May 96	V

FIGURE 2.1: *A project schedule.*

GANTT CHARTS

Gantt charts display planned and actual progress for a number of tasks against a horizontal time-scale. As well as showing when various tasks and activities are due to begin and reach completion, Gantt charts can identify the 'critical' links in a project. These are the points at which certain activities must be completed before others can start. If any of these 'critical' activities is delayed, the whole project will be put back.

Figure 2.2 shows a Gantt chart for a project to install a new computer system.

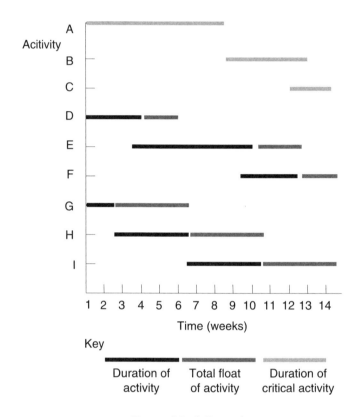

FIGURE 2.2: *A Gantt chart.*
SOURCE: C.D.J. Waters, 1991, *An Introduction to Operations Management,*
Addison - Wesley

CRITICAL PATH ANALYSIS

Critical path analysis shows the relationship between different activities more clearly than a Gantt chart. This technique, also known as network analysis, is a powerful tool for identifying the points at which bottlenecks are likely to occur in the project plan. The 'critical path' is the sequence of activities that has the least slack in it – the one which, if overrun, will have the greatest knock-on effect for the subsequent stages and for the project as a whole.

Once managers have identified the 'critical activities' of a project, they can allocate to them sufficient people and resources to ensure that the targets for those stages are met.

See the companion workbook *Managing People and Activities* for more on Gantt charts and CPA.

ACTIVITY 11

In a small group, draw up a plan for a real or imaginary project that you will undertake together. Ideas might include a plan for:

- an awards ceremony and dinner

- tour arrangements for a pop group

- producing an information pack or a video.

Produce your plan on a word processor. Use appropriate software to produce a project schedule or Gantt chart to include within your documentation.

Make notes in the box below.

Commentary...

When your project plan is complete, check that the plan includes:

- some objectives

- all the tasks that will have to be carried out to achieve the objectives

- the people who will carry out the tasks

- deadlines for completion of the tasks and the project as a whole.

summary

▶ Strategic plans are differentiated from other types of management plans because they are complex, uncertain and demand an integrated approach to managing the organisation.

▶ Operational plans are concerned with how the different functions of the organisation – marketing, personnel, production and so on – contribute to its strategic plan.

▶ Operational plans are frequently translated into action plans or personal development plans for individuals. These plans may form part of a performance appraisal system.

▶ Budgets have been described as 'the economic expressions of operational or strategic plans'. One of the major advantages of budgeting is that it demands a structured approach and forces precision in planning.

▶ Project management refers to the task of planning and controlling one-off 'projects'. Projects are different from other management activities because they have a single specific purpose and they have a definite start and end time.

Ideas into action

Objectives

After participating in this session, you should be able to:

▶ analyse how a vision, missions and an agreed set of values help to keep an organisation united and on course

▶ describe ways in which small organisations try to control growth

▶ identify the major differences between planning in the public and private sectors.

In working through this session, you will practise the following BTEC common skills:

Managing and developing self	✔
Working with and relating to others	✔
Communicating	✔
Managing tasks and solving problems	✔
Applying numeracy	
Applying technology	
Applying design and creativity	

Keeping the organisation on course

During the 1980s and 1990s, large organisations have adopted a number of ways of controlling their performance and of maintaining people's loyalty and commitment:

- providing a vision

- writing a mission

- defining business values.

These activities usually precede the formal planning process itself.

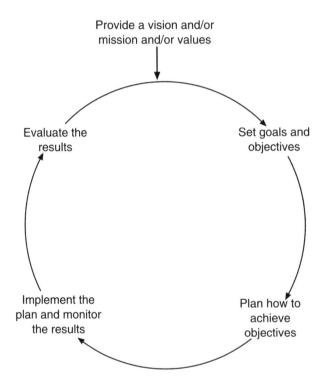

FIGURE 3.1: *The planning process.*

The results achieved by any organisation depend to a great extent on the quality of the mission, vision and values and the processes by which they are defined.

Not all organisations have a vision, mission and values; some have just two of these elements, others only one. At one extreme, missions and/or statements of values are written out formally on posters or on cards. At the other, nothing is written down at all; the leaders of the organisation just live by an agreed code of values and try to communicate these by their actions.

PROVIDING A VISION

Our conduct is influenced not by our experience but by our expectations.

George Bernard Shaw

Developing a vision is often the very first step of the planning process. It creates the energy needed to provide an organisation or a work team with its purpose and direction. A leader's ability to provide a vision for an organisation will influence people's commitment to attaining its targets and, ultimately, the quality of their performance. The purpose of a vision is to create challenge, excitement and a common direction for activities. With a vision, the leader provides a bridge from the present to the future.

ROCKWELL STANDARD

During the 1960s, Dr Edward Lindaman, then director of program control for the manufacture of Apollo spacecraft, continually emphasised: 'A fundamental determinant of how we choose to behave today is our conscious or below-conscious expectation of what the future could hold in store.'

He simulated pictures of what the moon landing would look like and had these mounted on the walls at Rockwell Standard so the work teams would 'get the picture'. Every Monday morning via an in-house TV network, Lindaman would interview a different team, demanding that they verbalise 'what the moon landing would be like for them'.

His insistence that everyone share and espouse a vision of a 'preferred future' kept people focused, energised and on target. It empowered them to do something that, in fact, had never been done before.

Source: Jim Clemmer and Art McNeil, 1989, *Leadership Skills for Every Manager,* Piatkus

---

This example shows how valuable it is for a leader to create a vision and then to encourage others in the team or the organisation to share this.

ACTIVITY 1

Write down what you understand by a 'vision' for an organisation.

SAT: allow 5 mins	?

| Communicating | ✔ |

Commentary...

We are not talking here about mystical apparitions or fantastic daydreams. By visions, we mean vivid pictures of what the organisation is trying to achieve. Understandably, not everyone is comfortable with the word 'vision'. People describe the word 'vision' in many different ways. Here are some examples:

- It is having an inspiring plan and living it; pursuing it enthusiastically.

- It's when the leader is buzzing with ideas. This generates enthusiasm and everyone knows what's expected.

- It is a self-fulfilling prophecy. Immense visions lead to immense possibilities. Poor visions have the opposite effect.

- A vision is a leap of the imagination – a leap of faith.

- A vision is a graphical and tangible picture of the future.

Visions can exist at any level. Here are some examples:

For a nation

> **I believe that this nation should commit itself to achieving the goal of landing a man on the moon and returning him safely to earth before this decade is out.**
>
> John F. Kennedy

For famine relief

> **Our concerts are keeping the starving alive. Now let us give them a life.**
>
> Bob Geldof

For an organisation

> **Our vision is to make the Post Office a world class benchmark of excellence in terms of total quality, customer initiatives, innovation, technology and product development.**
>
> Bill Cockburn, Post Office

For a team

> **I would like us to keep on finding better and better ways to get the job done.**
>
> Shift Manager, Royal Mail North East

When you think about it, most of things you have achieved were possible because, at a fundamental level, you had a vision or a picture of how things could be in the future.

ACTIVITY 2

Think of something that you have organised, created or achieved. You may, for example, have organised a swimming gala or a holiday, decorated your bedroom, written a piece of music or achieved something of which you were proud.

1. Write down what you did.

2. Explain when and how the idea first came to you.

3. Describe what motivated you and others to put the idea into practice.

SAT: allow 10 mins

Managing and developing self ✔

Commentary...

We cannot of course know what your example is, but here is someone talking about achieving a vision.

We weren't happy in that tiny terraced house in the town, it was pretty but much too small and cold. Then I was looking through a magazine one day and I saw a picture of a wonderful Scandinavian house built on a wooden frame, very spacious very elegant. It had all the environmental features, you know solar heating, complete draught proofing – extremely energy efficient. Then I thought that we could build one like that, it came to me that there was no reason why we couldn't have a house like that if we wanted one. Once I got the idea in my mind it would not go away and I found myself planning and working towards that end.

Psychologists tell us that it is easier to do things, particularly complex and challenging things, if we first of all try to see a picture of what it is we are trying to achieve. This is called **visualising,** and it is what successful organisations do for their employees. They imagine what the future is going to be like and paint a picture of this for their people.

For example if a small organisation wants to become known as 'world class', the leaders would visualise what it would be like to be in that league. They might see the impressive buildings, the boardroom, the shareholders' meetings, the soaring profits, the committed workforce, the delighted customers, the articles in glossy executive journals and so on. Leaders of successful organisations strive to:

- develop a clear vision that is consistent with the organisation's overall purpose and direction

- translate their vision into augmenting goals and objectives for the organisation

- encourage others to take ownership of the vision

- use the vision to inspire others and give them energy

- review and update their vision in response to changing circumstances.

Although everyone has their own way of looking at the future, the best visions are:

- different or innovative

- closely related to the work of the organisation

- easily understood by others

- believed and lived by the leader of the organisation

- adopted by the whole workforce.

WRITING A MISSION

Another way for organisations to communicate their purpose to their employees is through an agreed mission statement. In relatively few words, a **mission statement** defines the overall direction of the operation and also says something about its values.

When Sir Graham Day arrived at British Leyland in 1986, his whole strategy for change was built on a clear goal which amounted to a brief mission statement: to make money based on giving the customer what he's rarely had from a British car – complete satisfaction.

Here is a more formal mission statement written by a District Health Authority in the North-west of England:

> This Health Authority is committed to the promotion of health, the prevention of disease and disability and the treatment and support of the individual in the most appropriate way.
>
> **Principles:**
>
> 1. The health needs of the people of this county will determine the provision and priority of services within the resources available and within the constraints of national policies and priorities, taking into account the views of the consumer.
>
> 2. Primary health care will be the basis for meeting health care needs.
>
> 3. Hospital in-patient and out-patient (secondary care) provision will supplement primary health care.
>
> 4. Planning and provision of health care must be in partnership with other agencies.
>
> 5. Judgement on the efficiency and effectiveness of services will be on the basis of outcome.
>
> 6. We will build on the valuable contribution of staff, recognising their needs and contribution to the overall success of the Authority.

ACTIVITY 3

Managing tasks and solving problems ✔

Find a mission or a statement that has been written for an organisation you know well. If your work experience placement or college does not have one you could try:

- an NHS Trust or Health Authority

- the headquarters office of your Royal Mail division

- your local council

- a large retail store or supermarket

- your local Training and Enterprise Council (TEC).

Read through the mission state. Explain what it says about

- the purpose of the organisation

- the values of the organisation

- what the organisation could become in the future.

Commentary...

Many organisations have found over the last few years that defining, or redefining, their mission has revolutionised the way in which they operate. This process of going back to basics has been used to make organisations more customer focused, more quality conscious and more aware of the need to concentrate on what they do best. Peripheral tasks have in many cases been left to sub-contractors or incorporated in a new, completely separate business.

DEFINING BUSINESS VALUES

As we have seen, an organisation's values are sometimes expressed as part of an agreed mission statement. Vision and values are also interconnected; the vision of an organisation is shaped by its values and values will come alive through vision.

RICHARD GOSWELL

Richard Goswell, chief executive of Mercury One 2 One believes that the company's values are associated with enhanced business performance. 'Our values as a company have played a crucial role in our progress', he says. 'They may be less tangible than a mission statement but they are probably more real in the day-to-day working of 90 per cent of our staff.'

These values are as follows:

○ Giving **empowerment** and support for high expectations: we look for people who expect the best from themselves and we, in turn, expect the best from them.

○ Treating people as **individuals:** the business of Mercury One 2 One is all about people and their relationships in business, family and social life. Whether it is customer, supplier or a colleague, we always respect people and treat them as we would wish to be treated.

○ Respecting **families** and **communities:** we believe that supporting the growth and importance of family and community relationships is important to our business, important to our people and important in a broader social context.

○ Keeping things **straightforward** and better: all changes to our business must 'keep it simple' and be an improvement to our efficiency and cost base to meet all customer expectations and needs.

○ Being **ambassadors for communication:** 'Communication between people is the lifeblood of our business, so as a business, communication should be one of the things we are best at.'

Goswell says that no one in the organisation would pretend that these values are always reflected in everyday action. Rather they provide a 'target we should all be aiming at, a direction in which we should all be moving'.

Adapted from: Rob MacLachlan, 1995, 'The Pioneers who put people first' in *People Management*, 10 August

Properly chosen, values should:

○ create an atmosphere of trust – since everyone knows how they are expected to behave, managers can keep out of the way and let staff carry on

○ provide a clear focus for team or individual performance reviews

○ create a way of meeting qualitative rather than quantitative business objectives

○ help everyone to set priorities for their work

○ direct training and development activities

○ reduce politics and games playing

○ provide guidelines for selecting new employees

○ simplify rules and policies.

SAT:
allow 10 mins

Managing tasks and solving problems ✓

ACTIVITY 4

Read through the following statements.

(a) Only large organisations have visions.

(b) Visions are only valuable if they are translated into goals, objectives and plans.

(c) A mission and a vision are the same thing.

(d) A mission has to be written down and communicated to everyone in the organisation.

(e) Organisations can only identify their values if they have first defined their vision and their mission.

(f) Appropriate values let people know what is expected of them and helps them to set their priorities.

Which statements are true, and which are false? If you think a statement is false, explain why.

Commentary...

Statement (a) is false. Any organisation (or any department or team within an organisation) would find it useful to have a vision. However, providing a vision is a useful way for leaders of larger organisations to communicate a vivid picture of the future to staff who may be working in different geographical areas or business units.

Statement (b) is true. A vision is useless unless it is translated into plans for action.

Statements (c), (d) and (e) are false. A vision is 'a preferred picture of the future' while a mission is a statement of the organisation's overall purpose and direction. A mission does not have to be written down, but it does have to be communicated (and it is often easier to communicate a mission that is written down). Although some organisations like to have a vision, mission and values, many will only produce one or two of these elements.

Statement (f) is true. Values help people to work independently and to assess for themselves whether or not they are doing what the organisation requires of them.

Policies

Policies are developed within the framework of an organisation's objectives. They are general statements that guide or channel thinking when deciding which strategies to adopt to achieve objectives. Policies provide the foundation on which such decisions will be made, and they are usually based on ethics such as:

- maintaining standards of fair trading

- creating good relations with the general public, customers and suppliers

- providing fair conditions of employment

- producing only high-quality merchandise

- caring about the environment.

Some aspects of an organisation's policy may become so important that they become a 'hallmark' of that organisation. For example, Marks and Spencer has become inextricably linked with its policy of buying primarily from British suppliers and its 'no questions asked' exchange or refund policy. Similarly, the Body Shop owes a great part of its identity to its 'against animal testing' policy.

Policies can exist at all levels of the organisation, and range from major company policies through to departmental or functional policies. Examples include a recruitment policy, a pricing policy and an equal opportunities policy.

Because policies are often translated into rules, plans and procedures, they allow managers to delegate authority and still maintain control over what subordinates do. Policies deal with issues before they become problems and make it unnecessary to analyse every problem from first principles. For example, the guiding principles enshrined in a personnel policy may include:

○ advertising vacancies at the lower levels as widely as possible

○ giving priority to promotion from within the organisation

○ employing only professionally qualified accountants

○ permitting line managers to recruit staff up to a given level.

Some personnel policies are governed by government legislation, e.g. on equal pay, racial and sexual discrimination.

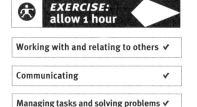

**EXERCISE:
allow 1 hour**

Working with and relating to others	✔
Communicating	✔
Managing tasks and solving problems	✔

ACTIVITY 5

One example of a company policy is its 'health and safety policy'. Collect a copy of your college's policy and discuss it with a partner. In the box below, note down the following:

○ the main features of the policy

○ the person or persons responsible for monitoring and enforcing it

○ some examples of any special arrangements that the college has made to ensure that health and safety standards are upheld.

Commentary...

Every organisation will have its own unique health and safety policy but the law states that they should all:

- ○ contain a general statement of intent

- ○ set out the main responsibilities of all managers and other employees

- ○ identify who is responsible for monitoring the policy

- ○ define the systems that allow safety standards to be maintained – these may include training, safe procedures, cleanliness, noise control, fire precautions and systems for reporting accidents.

POLICY IN THE PUBLIC SECTOR

Planning in the public sector is influenced to a large extent by the policies of the political party that governs the country and, to a much lesser extent, by the one that controls the local council. For example, Labour politicians tend to stress the need for welfare services and equity in the provision of those services. Conservative politicians, on the other hand, have traditionally placed emphasis on the free market and the control of public expenditure.

But policy is also often the product of expediency, forced on governments by domestic or international crises. A classic example is the extensive cuts in public spending forced on the Labour Government by the International Monetary Fund in the late 1970s. A more recent example is the introduction of the Council Tax, forced on the government by the unpopularity of rating system and, subsequently, the Poll Tax.

Although politicians on the Right both here and abroad often talk about 'rolling back the frontiers of the state' the reality is that the scope, extent and cost of government grew just as rapidly in the years of Thatcher or Bush as it did when Wilson or Kennedy were in power in the 1960s. This rapid growth in the extent of government policy and spending can be traced back to the Second World War.

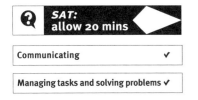

SAT: allow 20 mins

| Communicating | ✔ |
| Managing tasks and solving problems | ✔ |

ACTIVITY 6

Which government policies will be reflected in the business plans of organisations in:

(a) the National Health Service?

(b) education?

Commentary...

Business plans in the NHS have to reflect the following government policies:

- the requirement to put patients' needs first (the Patient Charter)

- the requirement to maintain and continuously improve standards of care (Clinical Audit)

- the introduction of the internal market and the requirement that providers should compete for contracts (*Working for Patients,* the government White Paper published in 1989)

- the option that is open to larger GP practices of becoming 'fundholders' – GP fundholders can now choose to provide services themselves, buy in from NHS providers or buy in from non-NHS providers.

In education, we see the influence of the following government policies on business plans:

- the National Curriculum and assessment tests

- the composition and role of the board of governors

- the requirement for in-service training for teachers

- regulations governing the delivery of sex education and religious education

- the imposition of local management for schools (LMS) which allows schools to manage their own budgets

- the choice for many schools to opt out of local authority control.

You may have mentioned other points that are not included here. The action that any government may decide to take in any of these or other areas is a reflection of its 'public policies'. Political parties set out their policies in their manifestos before an election, but these often evolve and change during the period of office.

It is becoming more common to make public policy work more effectively by using the kind of implementation process employed in the private sector. Policy is first translated into broad goals, which are further broken down into detailed objectives for achieving them. After that, managers decide on a strategy (or a plan of action) which sets out the method by which the objectives will be achieved.

Planning in large organisations

Large organisations face major planning decisions. They need to consider how to:

- structure and control the business

- link different parts of the business so that they can communicate effectively

- co-ordinate business operations in different units and geographical areas

- allocate resources to individual functions or business units, given their different and competing demands.

Large national or multinational organisations are likely to have a wide range of products or services, as they frequently operate in several markets simultaneously. The central strategic decisions in large organisations, therefore, tend to centre around the issues of structuring and controlling the business to achieve specific goals and objectives.

THE MULTIDIVISIONAL STRUCTURE

Federalism is an age old device for keeping the proper balance between big and small ... This is never easy because it means allowing the small to be independent while still being part of the larger whole.

Charles Handy, 1995, *The Empty Raincoat*, Arrow Business Books

Given the complexity of planning and control in large organisations, many of them have decided that they need to diversify their activities into several separate business divisions. Each unit takes responsibility for a particular product, process or geographical area. These divisions are frequently organised as separate business units, which in turn have their own functional structure, as shown in figure 3.2. The Royal Mail, with independent divisions in nine geographical areas is an example of an organisation that has altered its structure along these lines.

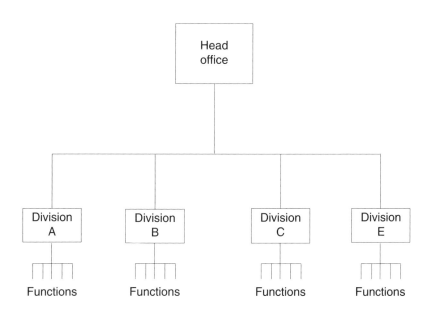

FIGURE 3.2: *A multidivisional structure.*

A major problem with this type of structure is deciding which functions should be placed under the control of corporate head office and which should be placed within the divisions. For example, should personnel management or financial services remain 'group' functions or should they devolve down into the units?

Nevertheless, experience has shown that the multidivisional structure has many advantages over the more traditional, hierarchical functional organisation. This structure is rapidly becoming the norm for the larger company all over the world.

How decentralisation influences planning

One of the main reasons why decentralisation has emerged as the dominant structure of most large business organisations is that this approach devolves the planning and control processes to the lower organisation levels. This, in turn, makes people feel more committed to achieving the organisation's purpose and goals.

Decentralisation focuses the efforts of managers directly on business performance and business results. Managers have to accept responsibility for poor, as well as for good, performance. They can no longer make excuses for not achieving targets. In a multidivisional structure, 'management by objectives' becomes fully effective. Managers of the business units know better than anyone else how their divisions are doing in relation to their objectives, and need no one else to tell them.

STRATEGIC CONTROL

Companies differ in the amount of freedom they give unit managers and the tightness of the controls imposed on them. However, most give central management the responsibility for the kind of core strategic decisions which determine the long-term future of the business as a whole. This ensures that these major decisions are made by those who have the widest experience and an overview of the interests of the whole organisation.

At General Electric, for example, only the president can make the decision to abandon a business or begin a new one. At General Motors, top management controls competition between the major units of the company by setting price ranges for each division's products.

In a decentralised multidivisional structure, one of the centre's key responsibilities is to assess the performance of divisions against their own business plans. The centre also has the role of allocating resources to the divisions; in this way, it can maintain an appropriate balance within the organisation as a whole. An important part of this process is setting and agreeing annual budgets.

The abandonment or relaxation of rules previously imposed from the centre gives many unit managers a feeling of freedom. Most find it invigorating to become involved in strategic decision making and to take responsibility for the results. However, some have difficulty in meeting the challenge of a decentralised structure. Tight control systems imposed by the centre can put enormous pressures on managers.

Others find the new responsibilities and accountabilities hard to live up to. Decentralisation can also bring excessive rivalry between the different business units, and people may develop a tendency to forget the overriding requirement of corporate loyalty.

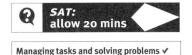

Q **SAT:**
allow 20 mins

Managing tasks and solving problems ✔

ACTIVITY 7

Using the matrix grid below, summarise some of the main benefits and problems of centralised and decentralised organisations.

	Benefits	Problems
Centralisation		
Decentralisation		

Commentary...

Your completed table may look something like this:

	Benefits	Problems
Centralisation	• Activities easy to co-ordinate • Easy to implement a common policy • Speedy communications • Fast decision making • Easy to specify and control strategy • Makes economies of scale possible	• Difficult to respond quickly to local conditions • Unit managers not so committed to strategy imposed from above • Difficult to develop management skills • Organisation top heavy and cumbersome
Decentralisation	• Units can respond quickly to specific customer demands • Managers in decentralised units are more committed to achieving objectives they have set for themselves • Provides opportunities for 'on the job' training of managers • Brings improved motivation and morale	• May be too much competition between units • Units may lose sight of the corporate 'purpose' • Difficult to split 'strategic' and 'operational' roles

Planning in small businesses

Small businesses tend to operate in a limited marketplace and are usually able to offer only a restricted range of products and services. Planning issues that are likely to be important for them therefore include:

- consolidating their position in the marketplace

- strategies for fighting off competitors

- raising capital – especially if a business seeks growth.

Planning decisions are likely to be strictly limited by the values and aspirations of the firm's founder or senior executives, who may also be the owners of the business. Even when the managers are not owners, it is likely that the values and expectations of the people who founded the business are still most influential.

In very small businesses, it is usually the owner who undertakes most of the responsibilities of management. If there is more than one person involved, there is often no clear definition of who is responsible for what. The operation is then run by the personal control and contact of one or two individuals.

The key problem tends to be that, if the business becomes too large for one or two people to control, it will cease to operate effectively. For small businesses, the vital planning issue is therefore the management of growth.

Fun Ts

Fun Ts started life in 1990, with Ceri and Jason, the two partners, personally buying in good quality T-shirts, dyeing, screen printing them and selling them on to retail outlets, organisations and individual customers. After two years, the numbers of orders had grown and the partners were working full time in the office, organising the activities of six production assistants. They were also spending a lot of time writing invoices, chasing payments, dealing with wages and going to Birmingham to liaise with Vanguard plc, the company buying 75 per cent of their product.

Things went reasonably well, until 1992, when three things happened to make the partners rethink their approach to running the business. First, Ceri and Jason's initial contract with Vanguard came to an end. Then, the lease on their premises ran out. Finally, all their employees joined a trades union. When the local organiser advised them that their pay was well below the national average they threatened industrial action.

Ceri and Jason now faced the kind of situation that brings many small businesses to an end. However they were not the kind of people to give up in a crisis.

ACTIVITY 8

In a group or with a partner, suggest some of the courses of action that Ceri and Jason might take to deal with these urgent problems. Summarise your ideas in the space below.

EXERCISE:
allow 1 hour

Working with and relating to others ✔

Managing tasks and solving problems ✔

Commentary...

What in fact happened was that the partners turned what looked like a disastrous situation into an opportunity to transform their business. What they did was by no means the only solution, however, and you may have thought of some equally valid ideas.

The partners approached their bank with a bold business plan that tackled all three problems. They would purchase a ten-year lease on a small factory unit, taking advantage of terms subsidised by the Regional Development Authority. They would invest in automated machinery to dye and process the T-shirts. They would sell their products directly to a wider range of customers, thus no longer supplying bulk buyers such as Vanguard.

They recognised that although they were good at planning and risk taking, a more professional approach had to be taken to functions such as industrial relations and accounting. They proposed setting up a proper organisational structure, with:

- a production manager, supervising the eight operatives and a part-time technician

- an office manager responsible for administration and supervising a clerk (dealing with purchases, sales and wages)

- a freelance consultant (subsidised by the local Training and Enterprise Council) advising on marketing, personnel and other matters on an irregular basis.

It was decided that Ceri would be in charge of day-to-day operations, while Jason would be responsible for finding new suppliers and new customers. He would also explore the possibilities of moving into new, but related, markets.

Planning in the public sector

The development of the techniques and language of planning has traditionally occurred in commercial organisations. However, these approaches are becoming increasingly important in the public sector.

This extract from an article in *The Economist* illustrates the extent to which the business approach has penetrated the public sector in the USA – in this case, the New York Police Department. At the time of writing, William Bratton is the commissioner of the NYPD.

> Like a freshly minted MBA student, Mr Bratton's talk is of re-engineering and decentralising, of empowerment and partnership. In his eyes, the NYPD is Crimebusters Inc.

> 'The profit I want is crime reduction', says Mr Bratton. By that measure his board (Mayor Rudolph Giuliani) and customers (the city's long suffering citizens) should be happy. In 1994, Mr Bratton's first year in office, he presided over a 12 per cent fall in recorded crime ... He reinvigorated New York's transit police by improving equipment but also through a dose of Druckerish 'management by objectives'.

The Economist, 29 July 1995, p.62

Likewise, in the UK, one of the key problems for public sector planners is that the distinction between 'public' and 'private' is becoming less well defined. This is happening in a number of distinct but related ways:

- many nationalised industries have become privatised

- public sector organisations engage in joint ventures with the private sector – 'quangos' such as Training and Education Councils (TECs) are an example of this

- public services like road maintenance are contracted out to private enterprise, yet the work is funded by taxation

- although some services (such as refuse collection) may be provided by public sector organisations, they will have had to tender competitively against private sector organisations to gain the contract to provide these services.

So, the services provided by the public sector are increasingly being exposed to the competitive marketplace. During the 1990s, we have seen this happening in health and social services which operate within a particular type of market system – sometimes called a **social market,** or **quasi-market**. Within this largely internal market, health authorities, fundholding GPs and social services authorities purchase services from competing provider units. This system has had a profound effect on the planning and delivery of health and social care; not least because it has forced providers to look at their services first and foremost from the point of view of the people who pay for it and use it.

One of the main aims of the reforms of the early 1990s was to improve health care by introducing an element of competition between providers. It was envisaged that this would encourage greater efficiency in the use of resources and make providers more aware of the needs of their consumers and purchasers.

Competition now exists in and between all sectors of the health service. In primary care, we see GPs competing with each other for patients or tendering for contracts to provide certain specialist services. Hospitals compete across boundaries and for referrals from GPs; they also compete with primary or community health care to provide, for example, mental health services. In community and social care, there is competition between nursing homes and between community care and social services.

Despite this inevitable outcome of the legislation, there is a growing belief that cut-throat competition is not the best way to ensure high quality care and value for money. Managers, as well as practitioners, are coming to recognise that competition tempered by co-operation can lead to a less destructive but no less efficient way of planning and providing services.

In this time of turbulent change, all public sector organisations are using the planning process to help them to gain a deeper understanding of the trends and influences which are shaping their role and activities. Many organisations and departments are finding it helpful to:

- redefine their purpose (often by means of an agreed 'mission' statement)

- identify their stakeholders' expectations

- identify their internal and external customers and their requirements

- anticipate the forces and influences that will shape the nature and role of their service

- redefine their 'product' or the nature of their services.

Differences between the private and public sectors

Despite the blurring of the boundary between the different sectors, there remain many factors which make management planning within the public sector very different from the private sector.

> **Public sector bodies like ours derive their powers ultimately from Parliament, to whom, in turn, they are ultimately accountable.**
>
> Employment services manager

> **Our service exists to serve the whole of society – it cannot choose to opt out, as a private company can opt out, of operating in a particular section of the market.**
>
> DSS Manager

> **Private sector managers are accountable mainly to their own line managers and, ultimately, to their shareholders. By contrast, our list of stakeholders is almost overwhelming: doctors, nurses, patients, carers, taxpayers, the government, the health authority, the board, interest groups and so on.**
>
> Financial Director in an NHS Trust

We can't make plans and take decisive action like managers in private companies. The democratic process and formal decision-making procedures put tremendous constraints on what we can achieve.

District Manager in the Post Office

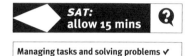

SAT:
allow 15 mins

Managing tasks and solving problems ✔

ACTIVITY 9

In the box below, list the things which you consider differentiate planning in the public sector from that in the private sector.

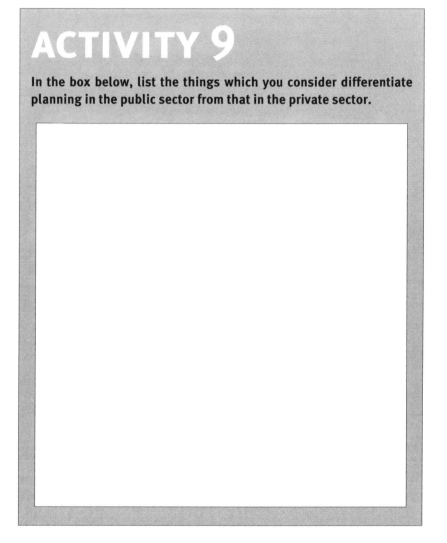

Commentary...

Several arguments are usually put forward to illustrate the uniqueness of the public sector. It is important for managers to identify what these differences are, so that they know where they should focus their attention when considering strategic and operational plans.

You may have included some of the following points:

- Long-term planning in the public sector is often constrained by the short-term considerations of politicians.

- Non-commercial areas of the public sector are primarily funded by taxation, and not by charging for services.

- The legislation governing the way in which much of the public sector functions is limited by statute.

- Certain goods have to be provided by the state; defence, law and order and street lighting are enjoyed collectively. In theory, they are equally available to all, and the provision of such public goods cannot be left to the marketplace.

- Accountability is a constant factor in public organisations; the activities of the public sector are subject to continual scrutiny from politicians, pressure groups, taxpayers and voters.

Given that important dissimilarities do exist, a very specialised style of behaviour is required to bring about good planning in the public sector. Although there is much that the public sector can learn from private enterprise, particularly in terms of how to respond to the needs of the market, entrepreneurial values cannot simply be imported lock, stock and barrel.

summary

▶ Developing a vision is often the first step of the planning process. It creates the energy needed to provide an organisation or a work team with its purpose and direction. Other ways in which an increasing number of organisations communicate their purpose to the workforce is through an agreed 'mission statement' or 'values'.

▶ Policies are developed within the framework of an organisation's objectives. They are general statements that guide or channel thinking in deciding which strategies to adopt to achieve objectives. Policies provide the foundation on which such decisions will be made, and they are usually based on ethical considerations.

▶ Given the complexity of planning and control in large organisations, many of them have decided that they need to break their activities into several separate business divisions. Each unit takes responsibility for a particular product, process or geographical area.

▶ In a decentralised multidivisional structure, one of the centre's key responsibilities is to assess the performance of divisions against their own business plans. The centre also has the role of allocating resources to the divisions.

▶ Small businesses tend to operate in a limited marketplace and are usually able to offer only a restricted range of products and services. Planning issues that are likely to be important for them therefore include: consolidating their position in the marketplace, strategies for fighting off competitors and raising capital.

▶ The services provided by the public sector are increasingly being exposed to the competitive marketplace. This means that they have been forced to adopt many of the characteristics traditionally associated with market-driven organisations.

▶ Public sector organisations are using the planning process to help them to gain a deeper understanding of the trends and influences which are shaping their role and activities.

Planning for change

Objectives

After participating in this session, you should be able to:

▶ examine some of the pressures which force businesses to plan for change

▶ identify and categorise the external forces that exert an influence on organisational plans

▶ analyse the factors within the organisation that help or hinder future development

▶ explain a method for identifying the strengths and weaknesses of businesses

▶ identify the risks associated with different approaches to change.

In working through this session, you will practise the following BTEC common skills:

Managing and developing self	✔
Working with and relating to others	✔
Communicating	✔
Managing tasks and solving problems	✔
Applying numeracy	
Applying technology	
Applying design and creativity	

The pressure for change

A speech made by John F. Kennedy echoes one of the main themes of this workbook:

> **Change is the law of life, and those who look only to the past or present are certain to miss the future.**
>
> John F. Kennedy, 1963, Frankfurt

Planning is the way in which managers develop and change their goals and ensure that these goals are achieved.

The plans that a business makes are influenced by a range of forces in the external environment. Those forces are continually changing, and the speed at which they change is increasing all the time. Advanced computer systems, satellite communications, the European Union, the development of the role of women, the decline of trades unions are just some of the innovations that have made an enormous difference to the way in which businesses operate.

But there is in fact nothing particularly sinister about change. Organisations which make it their business to be informed about change and are prepared to respond quickly to external forces are those which stand the greatest chance of surviving. The ones that actively embrace change and participate in bringing it about are those which stand the greatest chance of thriving.

In his book *The Age of Unreason*, Charles Handy (BBC Business Books, 1991) tells the story of the Peruvian Indians who, seeing the sails of the Spanish invaders on the horizon, put this down to freak weather conditions and went about their business as usual. Those Spanish invaders eventually laid waste the entire Peruvian civilisation.

Both 'sudden' and 'creeping' changes affect organisations. The sudden, obvious ones tend to provoke a knee-jerk reaction if they are not spotted in advance and planned for. They can cause problems of disruption, mistrust and, sometimes, panic. Creeping change may not be noticed until it is too late, unless there is a mechanism for monitoring the environment, recognising when change is happening and responding to this with appropriate decisions, plans and actions.

Again in *The Age of Unreason,* Handy describes a frog that is put in cold water. If the water is slowly heated up, it will not move, until eventually it allows itself to be boiled alive. Organisations that want to avoid the fate of the Peruvian Indians and the boiling frog have to learn to look for – and welcome – continuous change.

ACTIVITY 1

This activity may require you to do some research. You may, for example, have to look through back issues of the financial and business press.

1. Name one well-known organisation that initiated and managed change well. Give reasons for your answer.

2. Name another organisation that has had difficulties in initiating and managing change. Again, give reasons for your answer.

Commentary...

You may have considered many different companies when making your selection. We give two examples here.

The Rover Group has successfully changed from a loss-making car manufacturer with an out-dated model range and a reputation for poor quality. It now has a modern range of high-quality vehicles and is making profits.

IBM experienced great difficulty in adapting to the market shift from large mainframe and mini computer installations to desktop microcomputers. Although the company has now successfully come through a painful period of transition, the enormous losses and dented prestige of the dark years could have been avoided by a less ostrich-like approach.

These examples show how important it is for organisations to be receptive to change and to plan change carefully.

ELEMENTS OF CHANGE

We now look at some of the main areas where businesses are experiencing change during the second half of the 1990s.

The effects of **competitor activities** are a major consideration for an organisation's planners. Strategic plans must be designed to ensure that an organisation achieves and keeps 'competitive advantage'.

All businesses are to a greater or lesser extent influenced and affected by the **competitive environment**. In the 1970s and 1980s, most UK organisations viewed the home market as the area within which they would do battle. The situation in the late 1990s, however, is totally different; national boundaries no longer form the barrier to trade that they once did. Now competition from overseas represents a substantial threat, while many businesses set their sights on exploiting opportunities in the global market.

EXERCISE:
allow 1 hour

Managing tasks and solving problems ✔

ACTIVITY 2

Resource 1 (at the back of this workbook) describes how First Direct has tried to attain an advantage over its competitors in the tough market for financial services.

Read Resource 1 carefully and analyse how the organisation's strategy has been designed to achieve a considerable advantage for First Direct. You may find it useful to collect additional publicity material from newspaper advertisements or from the company itself.

Use the following questions as a guide.

(a) What is the basis of First Direct's competitive advantage?

(b) In what major area does it hope to constitute a threat to its competitors?

In writing your answer, pick out some elements of its current strategy.

Commentary...

First Direct is in direct competition with other banks. Here are the main points that you should have covered in your analysis:

- The basis of First Direct's competitive advantage is speed, convenience, value for money and quality of service.

- It hopes to constitute a threat to its competitors in quality of service.

- Elements of its current strategy include providing excellent customer service and gaining commitment from the workforce.

Many companies have identified **quality** as being the only area where they can steal a march on their competitors. One of the leading 'quality gurus', W. Edwards **Deming**, who worked with Japanese firms in some of the earliest post-war quality programmes, defined quality as 'continually satisfying customer requirements'.

If customers feel that the product or service meets their needs, they are likely to buy more. Customers are therefore the life blood of any organisation; they are the reason for both survival and growth. Companies must develop a **customer focus**. So it is the task of planners to identify ways in which customer requirements can be identified and met. The first stage in making sure that customers' needs are satisfied is to identify exactly who the customers are.

External customers are the people who buy products or use services and may include:

- members of other organisations – customers for a firm of printers are local companies who require printed material

- supermarkets, agents or distributors, if products or services are distributed through some kind of network.

In many larger organisations, the **consumer** who uses the product may receive it from the external customer, rather than buying it directly. Organisations that want to achieve peak performance have to remember that the requirements of both customers and consumers have to be met.

	Tour firm	**Food firm**	**Hospital**	**Toy shop**
External customer	travel agent	supermarket	doctor	adult
Consumer	tourist	shopper	patient	child

FIGURE 4.1: *Examples of external customers and consumers.*

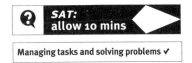

Managing tasks and solving problems ✔

ACTIVITY 3

Who are the external customers and consumers of the following businesses?

	Publisher	**Dairy firm**	**Pharmaceuticals manufacturer**
External customer			
Consumer			

Commentary...

You should have noted:

	Publisher	Dairy firm	Pharmaceuticals manufacturer
External customer	book shops/ clubs	Milk Marketing Board/ supermarkets	doctors and chemists
Consumer	readers	general public	patients or carers

Departments, teams and sections also have customers within the larger organisation: **internal customers**.

- When an assistant types a report for a manager, the manager is the internal customer.

- When a radiographer prepares an X-ray, the customer is the doctor who requested the X-ray.

- In a manufacturing company, the packers are the internal customers of the production line.

ACTIVITY 4

Find out some of the ways in which organisations determine what their customers and consumers require from them. You can do this by thinking of your own experience as a consumer, by reading books on marketing (including *Market Relations*, a companion volume in this series) that you will find in the library and by talking to people who work in business.

EXERCISE: allow 1 hour

Communicating ✔

Managing tasks and solving problems ✔

Commentary...

You may have listed some these methods:

- analysing customer complaints

- marketing research

- asking external customers and consumers for oral or written feedback

- holding meetings with important customers to discuss their needs

- encouraging staff to make the most of every opportunity to talk to external customers

- setting up project teams or 'quality circles' drawn from different departments within an organisation

- holding regular cross-departmental meetings to discuss problems and issues.

So, the key to finding out what customers and consumers want is to listen to them.

Because customer requirements and the business environment are constantly changing, a business that wants to achieve quality can never stand still. The goods and services provided by organisations must be continuously improved to meet changing standards and growing customer expectations.

Many businesses have adopted a policy of **continuous improvement**. Managers in business that have joined the quality movement use the **quality improvement cycle** to guide them in their planning. The five key phases are shown in figure 4.2. Organisations can never achieve perfect quality – what characterises quality programmes is their commitment to continual change and improvement.

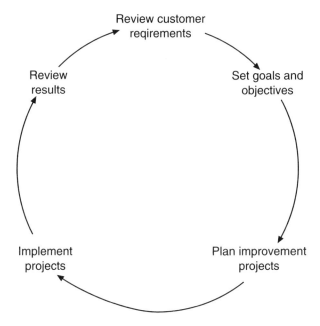

FIGURE 4.2: *The quality improvement cycle.*

External influences

All managers – in commerce, industry, public or voluntary sectors – have to take into account the influences exerted on their business by the external environment. If their plans are to be meaningful and practical, they need to recognise how these external forces affect the decisions they make and the objectives and tactics they identify.

Stories of how environmental pressure can result in business success or failure are all around us. It is estimated that Bill Gates, chairman, Chief Executive Officer and founder of the software company Microsoft, made $15 million by predicting the PC revolution. By contrast, Ladbrokes' failure to anticipate the effects (on its betting shop business) of the National Lottery, meant that its profits dropped by approximately £10 million in six months and it was forced to make 300 redundancies.

Leaders and managers must, therefore, make their plans in the context of the external environment. Although in many cases little can be done to eliminate or modify those forces, much can be done to reduce their adverse effects. Once managers have identified the main characteristics of the environment in which their organisations operate, they must then minimise the threats from the external environment and move on to create new opportunities within it.

Figure 4.3 shows the six main areas that influence the structure and the growth of any organisation. These six categories are easily remembered by the acronym **PESTLE**.

FIGURE 4.3: *PESTLE.*

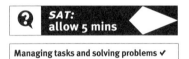

Managing tasks and solving problems ✔

ACTIVITY 5

Here are six factors which exert an influence over the development of businesses. Identify each one as political, economic, social, technological, legal or environmental.

(a) Regulations governing the employment of part-time staff

(b) The balance of trade

(c) Satellite communications systems

(d) The composition and structure of a country's population

(e) Green consumerism

(f) Financial deregulation.

Commentary...

You should have noted that factor (a) is a legal influence, (b) economic, (c) technical, (d) social, (e) environmental and (f) is a political influence.

If you have already worked through the companion BTEC workbooks in this series you will know that it is possible to categorise the business environment in a number of ways.

- In *Market Relations,* the model is called **DEPICTS:** demographic, economic, political, infrastructure, competitive, technological, socio-legal.

- Elsewhere you may see **DEEPEST:** demographic, epidemiological, ethical and legal, political, economic, social, technological.

- The simplest is **PEST:** political, economic, social, technological.

So you can see that the headings themselves are not sacrosanct; they are merely a means of highlighting a wide range of factors that may be relevant to the planning process. Furthermore, the headings are not mutually exclusive. Some of the factors that planners identify may have, for example, both social and legal dimensions. Planners usually harness them as a stimulus for thought rather than a rigorous classification.

Here, we use PESTLE to analyse the general business environment in the mid to late 1990s. It is by no means comprehensive – your assignment will provide an opportunity for you to add more specific items to this list.

Remember that the reason for doing an environmental analysis is:

- to identify those features that pose an actual or potential threat and plan how to overcome or avoid these

- to identify those features that represent opportunities and plan how to make the most of these.

POLITICAL FACTORS

The attitudes and actions of our political leaders and legislators affect virtually every aspect of life and every business organisation. Government can promote business by stimulating economic expansion and development, by subsidising selected industries, by giving tax advantages in certain situations, by supporting research and development and even by protecting businesses through special tariffs.

Now consider two examples of political factors that have influenced organisational development. During the late 1980s, the government brought import prices down, reduced taxation and introduced financial deregulation. This unleashed an avalanche of credit and consumption rose because people could borrow heavily. This triggered the housing boom and a spiral of credit and spending. Demand was skewed towards imports and luxury goods like yachts, high performance cars, race horses, fine art and designer clothes.

In the early 1990s, the capacity of local authorities for revenue raising and autonomous spending decisions was severely curtailed. Areas such as education and housing were progressively transferred to opted-out trusts. Many of the remaining authorities' operations had to be contracted out to external suppliers.

A political factor that is exercising many businesses at the time of writing is the high probability (at least with the bookmakers!) that the Labour Party will win the 1996 (or 1997) general election. The political programme that Tony Blair proposes could bring far-reaching changes to the business environment.

- **Europe:** the Labour Party proposes to adopt the Social Chapter. This set of principles about fair treatment at work would bring benefits for employees but the Conservatives claim it will load additional costs on to employers and destroy jobs.

- The **minimum wage:** Tony Blair is under pressure from the unions to impose a minimum wage of about half the national hourly wage. Again, planners will have to decide how to absorb or deal with the cost of this policy.

- **Nationalisation:** Labour has abandoned plans to re-nationalise the privatised utilities. Instead it promises to regulate them more rigorously. Planners in the water, gas and electricity companies have to identify ways of countering this threat to the freedoms they have so far enjoyed.

ECONOMIC FACTORS

Developments in the national and international economy have a significant impact on both business organisations and public service organisations.

Changes in government spending policies affect not only the supply of public services but also the demand for goods used in servicing public sector and welfare organisations. Cutbacks in public sector spending can also result in lower demand for private sector goods, services and resources. By contrast, any increase in public spending means that public services can expand, jobs will be created or saved and those who supply goods and services to the public services will flourish.

Most businesses await the Chancellor's annual Budget with avid interest because of the wide-ranging effects that this statement has on their development prospects.

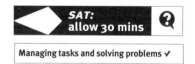

SAT: allow 30 mins

Managing tasks and solving problems ✔

ACTIVITY 6

The economic measures announced by Kenneth Clark in his November 1995 budget included:

- a 1.6 per cent increase in the budget of the national health service

- cuts in the road building programme

- a 3 per cent cut in the Department of National Heritage budget

- a 4 per cent cut in the excise duty on whisky.

For each measure, suggest which organisations will be affected and how. Consider both the organisations that are threatened by the measures and those which stand to benefit or might see the move as an opportunity. Summarise your ideas in the box below.

Commentary...

The real increase in NHS spending is good news for health authorities, NHS Trusts, GP fundholding and non-fundholding practices. Voluntary organisations and private providers will also be able to develop their services as a result of this measure because health service purchasers are being encouraged to contract services outside the NHS itself. Pharmaceutical companies, chemists shops and companies providing the NHS with medical supplies, equipment and services also stand to gain from the Chancellor's announcement.

Cuts in road spending pose a threat to road construction companies and road haulage companies. Businesses involved in providing other forms of transport, railway companies and bicycle manufacturers, on the other hand, might see this measure as a business opportunity.

The cut in the heritage budget can be seen as a threat by the Arts Council, historic buildings, monuments, museums, galleries and libraries. It means that theatres, arts centres and community groups are faced with grant reductions. Organisations which might see the reduction of the heritage budget as an opportunity are those who can offer alternative forms of entertainment or ways of experiencing our cultural heritage. Television companies, producers of CD-ROMs or organisations who can offer Internet services may develop themselves to fill the gap left when such cuts take effect.

Both whisky manufacturers and drinkers should welcome the announcement of 27 pence off a bottle of whisky. However, the beer industry was disappointed that the Chancellor did not impose a similar cut on the duty on beer. British beer, it is argued, is much more expensive than French beer because the duty is seven times higher. As a result, both the Exchequer and the industry lose millions of pounds every year as a result of 'cross border shopping'.

It is one of management's tasks to plan for and respond to these types of changes and their likely effects on the organisations they manage.

Another important influence on organisation is government fiscal and tax policies; the economic impact of these factors is tremendous. If taxes on business products are high, the incentive to go into business or stay in it drops, and investors will look elsewhere to invest their capital. If taxes are levied on sales, prices will rise and people will tend to buy less.

The balance between the domestic and overseas components of national income is vital when considering the prospects for UK companies. Where there is falling domestic demand for UK products, companies can offset this by planning for higher exports. Rising domestic demand can cause them to divert selling from the 'hard' overseas markets to 'soft' domestic ones. If domestic demand is unsatisfied by home production, it is likely to suck in imports – with implications for the balance of trade.

The balance of trade is not important on its own account but because of its consequences for interest rates, exchange rates and inflation. All these variables are interconnected, and each one has a different importance for individual organisations and different parts of the economy.

THE SINGLE EUROPEAN MARKET

In 1992, the creation of the single European market created immense opportunities and benefits for member states, businesses and people. Many strategists were quick to recognise opportunities for:

- ⚪ expanding into overseas markets – including exporting goods and services and opening factories or offices abroad

- ⚪ developing new products – expansion can also involve manufacturing new products or developing services to meet demand in overseas markets

- ⚪ job creation – the European market involves job opportunities and mobility for workers as well as firms.

The benefits for firms already operating in Europe include savings by the removal of barriers which formerly hindered new market entrants and obstructed competition.

Among the threats created by the single European market is the fact that it is now easier for foreign companies to compete for business in the UK. Business strategists have to be aware of where this new competition is likely to come from, what form it may take and they must plan how to protect themselves from the potential danger.

SOCIAL ENVIRONMENT

Organisations are complex social structures which themselves operate in a wider complex social environment. When planning, managers must always take into account social structure, social change and the attitudes, desires, expectations, and customs of the people who live in the social environment. The interweaving and complexity of these elements are such that comprehending, anticipating and preparing for them can be extremely challenging.

The composition and structure of a country's population have considerable implications for all business organisations. **Demographic factors** include the characteristics of the target customer or client group, such as sex ratio, ethnic composition, family size, life expectancies and so on.

As population changes work through to the economy, they create opportunities for developing new markets and products, while some existing ones will decline and disappear. A prime example of this is the development of goods and services aimed primarily at the over fifties – people who have retired early, have plenty of leisure time and a good pension. In the public sector, changes in the age distribution of the population lead to new demands on the education, health and social services.

Social trends such as changes in the role of women have had far-reaching implications for markets, products and organisational structures. Women are now becoming a significant economic and political force so that their wishes and requirements have to be taken into account by managers who are planning strategic organisational change.

Other trends that businesses have to be aware of when making plans for the future can be conveniently categorised under the heading **'lifestyle'**.

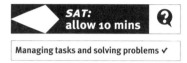

Managing tasks and solving problems ✓

ACTIVITY 7

In the box below, note some common recent lifestyle changes that might have had an effect on the business decisions and directions taken by many businesses.

Consider, in particular, changing attitudes and trends in:

- **food**
- **drink**
- **health**
- **leisure.**

Commentary...

Your ideas will depend to a great extent on your preferred lifestyle and experiences to date. However, some common trends that businesses may need to analyse closely are given here:

- **Food:** a desire for healthy eating, interest in vegetarian cooking, eating fast or convenience food, entertaining friends, meals for single or older people living on their own

- **Drink:** the growing preference for non/low alcoholic drinks, glucose drinks for cyclists or weight trainers, a move away from drinking beer towards lager, or red wine for supposed health benefits

- **Health:** awareness of the need to combat stress and take more exercise, interest in alternative medicines, increase in the incidence of health problems related to pollution

- **Leisure:** trends in clothes, music and other forms of entertainment such as the use of CD-ROM.

These and many other social trends are considered by business managers when they make decisions about the development of their products and services.

TECHNOLOGICAL FACTORS

There has always been a strong tie between business and technology. We have seen this throughout history – from the invention of the loom and the printing press to the design of the threshing machine and the tractor.

To survive in a changing world every business must keep abreast of the technology applicable to its products and services and to its methods of operation. To do otherwise is to risk destruction as competitors take advantage of new developments.

FEDERAL EXPRESS

Federal Express could not have become 'fast cycle' without modern technology. It is a parcel delivery business that guarantees that any package sent within the USA will be delivered by 10.30 a.m. the next day. To do this, the company has its own planes and vehicles and has invested heavily in information technology.

As soon as a parcel is received, a bar code is put on it giving details of its destination. This is used to control the parcel throughout the journey. The bar code can be read by a handheld scanning pen called a super tracker. A parcel tracking system called Cosmos scans the bar code at each stage on the journey and re-routes it. The company also has its own weather analysis centre and satellite television for communicating with employees.

Other parcel companies were forced to become fast cycle to compete with Federal Express. For example, in the ten years to 1989, TNT UK grew from £5 million turnover to £300 million and increased its staff from 500 to 8,000.

Source: Carol Cashmore and Richard Lyall, 1991, *Business Information Systems and Strategies,* Prentice Hall

ACTIVITY 8

EXERCISE:
allow 2 hours

Managing tasks and solving problems ✔

First Direct is an example of a fast-cycle company: a business that uses technology to enable it to meet customers' needs in the shortest possible time. Many companies use computer systems to enable them to speed up their manufacturing process or provide a quicker service. Look in the information systems section of your library and find out what the following terms mean:

- **just-in-time (JIT)**

- **material requirements planning (MRP I)**

- **manufacturing resource planning (MRP II)**

- **distribution resource planning (DRP)**

- **electronic point of sale (EPOS).**

Commentary...

You should have been able to gather quite a lot of information on the different systems. Here is just a brief explanation of each term.

Just-in-time (JIT) attempts to produce components and products as they are required by customers rather than in advance. The idea is to abolish finished goods stock and production work in progress. JIT systems are usually (but not necessarily) computerised.

Material requirements planning (MRP I) is a computer system that 'explodes' a finished product backwards in terms of its material content. When a customer orders a product, this has to be broken down into its components and raw materials for ordering purposes. Some materials have to be ordered straight away, others can be ordered later so as to arrive in time for the production process.

Manufacturing resource planning (MRP II) is an integrated decision-support system for planning, management and control that covers three activities: customer orders, materials and components management and use of resources. The system creates production schedules using a forecast of customer orders and details of lead times and capacity constraints.

Distribution resource planning (DRP) is also based on the concept of reducing stock and pulling goods through as they are ordered by customers. The techniques are exactly the same as those used in MRP except that they are applied in the distribution aspect of an operation rather than in manufacturing.

Electronic point of sale (EPOS) uses a bar code reader at the checkouts in supermarkets (and other stores) with computer systems to eliminate the need to record stock movements and write orders by hand. Thus the shop should never be out of stock and food should always be fresh.

During the 1980s and 1990s, systems such as those described above have created new business possibilities, improved general efficiency and have frequently resulted in substantial cost savings. But organisations that have been slow to identify the opportunities presented by 'fast cycle' or other forms of new technology have faced substantial reductions in both market share and profits.

LEGAL FACTORS

The legal environment is that complex mix of laws, regulations and government agencies and their actions, which affect all kinds of organisations to varying degrees. Every manager in every kind of organisation has to take account of a mass of laws, official regulations, rules and guidelines when making decisions about the future. Some laws set out to protect employees, consumers and communities. Others are designed to make contracts enforceable and to protect property rights.

For example, in 1994 the House of Lord ruled that UK laws on part-time workers' rights were in breach of European law. The government subsequently ruled that part-timers should receive the same employment protection as full-time employees. One of the main implications of this ruling is that women who work part-time and become pregnant are now eligible for exactly the same maternity benefits as full-time employees. They are entitled to maternity leave, maternity pay and have the right to return to work after their confinement. Planners have always had to plan for the contingency that their full-time female employees may become pregnant; they now have to allow for the fact that pregnant part-time workers may also bring added costs.

EXTERNAL INFLUENCES

EXERCISE:
allow 2 hours

Managing tasks and solving problems ✔

ACTIVITY 9

Use journals, books and other available resources to research the European legislation that has influenced, or will influence, the way that UK businesses operate and develop. Write up your findings in the form of a report (of some 1000 words). You may wish to consider using the following headings:

- **Part-time workers**

- **Health and safety**

- **Working conditions**

- **Trading standards**

- **Consumer protection.**

ENVIRONMENTAL FACTORS

Businesses do not have a natural propensity to look after the environment. It is more natural for them to cut costs and increase profits. But those that now choose to ignore their consumers' political and environmental demands are placing the very future of their businesses in jeopardy. This clearly imposes a new kind of difficulty on companies; one that most multinationals are taking seriously.

THE BRENT SPAR CASE

In June 1995, a consumer boycott forced Royal Dutch/Shell to drop plans to dispose of Brent Spar, a disused off-shore oil storage buoy, by sending it to the bottom of the Atlantic Ocean. The boycotters had refused to buy the firm's petrol on the grounds that they did not want Shell to turn the ocean into a rubbish dump. Activists from Greenpeace, in a brilliantly organised campaign, landed on the buoy by helicopter to prevent it from being sunk.

Shell thought it had explained the merits of its case thoroughly enough, but evidently it had not. The company maintained all along that if it was not to be buried at sea, Brent Spar would have to be disposed of on land – an option that was likely to be dirtier and more dangerous.

Failure to anticipate the adverse reaction across most of Europe was a blunder that resulted in an expensive public relations disaster. Furthermore, its decision to back down infuriated the British government, which alone had defended Shell's plans for burying the rig at sea.

Source: 'After Shell's Climbdown' in *The Economist,* 24 June 1995, p.15

Recent years have witnessed the emergence of green consumerism as the business response to growing environmental awareness. It is no longer left to the leaders of Greenpeace and Friends of the Earth to express their concern over conserving natural resources or using technologies and products that minimise the pollution of the environment.

ACTIVITY 10

In a group, discuss the national retail organisations that have integrated environmental consciousness as part of a broader corporate marketing strategy. What strategies have these organisations introduced in response to the 'green' factor? Note your ideas in the box below.

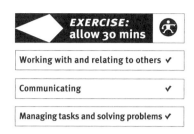

EXERCISE:
allow 30 mins

| Working with and relating to others ✔ |
| Communicating ✔ |
| Managing tasks and solving problems ✔ |

Commentary...

You may have mentioned shops and supermarket chains such as The Body Shop, Tesco and Sainsbury. For organisations like these, doing business in an increasingly 'green' world means:

- anticipating demand for new environment friendly products

- designing safer, healthier and less polluting products and packages

- developing less polluting manufacturing facilities

- minimising hazardous waste

- conserving non-renewable natural resources

- protecting the environment

- safeguarding worker and public health.

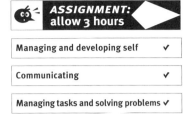

ACTIVITY 11

Write a 2000-word report that analyses the main factors in the external environment that influence the way in which one public sector or private sector industry will develop over the next few years.

For your research, you should find plenty of information in the textbooks and management journals in your college library. You may find it interesting to research an industry in which you would like to work, e.g. engineering, journalism, tourism or leisure.

When your report is finished, it should be organised in terms of the PESTLE headings discussed earlier. In thinking through your analysis:

- identify some aspects of Conservative or Labour policy that are likely to affect your chosen industry in the next few years

- identify some economic factors that may influence the way that businesses in the industry will develop

- consider which social trends managers will have to be aware of as they develop products and services

- identify any technological factors relevant in the industry

- consider which new laws planners will have to be aware of

- consider which environmental factors they will have to take into account.

Your finished report should be word processed. It should be supported by appropriate data. Note your main points in the box below.

Internal influences

The complexities of planning change in large-scale businesses have led many managers, writers and observers to take a growing interest in the concept of organisational culture. This is how Charles Handy describes the concept of culture.

> **In organisations there are deep set beliefs about the way work should be organised, the way authority should be exercised, people rewarded, people controlled. What are the degrees of formalisation required? How much planning and how far ahead? What combination of obedience and initiative is looked for in subordinates?**

> Charles Handy, 1993, *Understanding Organisations,* 4th edn, Penguin

Managers need to understand the predominant culture and how this can act as a constraint on organisational plans. Experience has shown that there is a greater likelihood of achieving change if efforts are directed at culture rather than by using structural or procedural methods alone.

The next case study illustrates the fundamental importance of taking culture into account when planning strategic change.

CMB PACKAGING

CMB Packaging was formed in 1989 as an Anglo-French merger of the Metal Box Company and Carnaud. There were good reasons to be optimistic about the merger; Metal Box was a market leader in the UK while Carnaud was strong in the rest of Europe.

In the event, the real world interfered with the vision and highlighted differences in management philosophy. At the top level, the president of Carnaud, Jean-Marie Descarpenteries, was described as 'flamboyant, a showman, an archetypal Frenchman, full of French management school ideas, like the inverted pyramid with customers at the top and management at the bottom ...'

By contrast, the Metal Box group operated with typical British top-down, centralised management approach. This clash of cultures led to indecision about the company's strategy and ultimately to declining performance.

Source: *The Times,* 12 September 1991

The success of an organisation seems to depend on establishing and maintaining an atmosphere or shared 'culture' that is appropriate to the work involved and which helps members of the organisation to value and aim for the same things.

FOUR TYPES OF ORGANISATION

In his paper 'How to Describe your Organisation' Roger Harrison (*Harvard Business Review*, Sept–Oct 1972) distinguishes between four types of organisation that differ in terms of their organisational culture – the things they value, the way that they handle change, their attitudes towards customers and so on.

- power oriented
- role oriented
- achievement oriented
- support oriented.

Table 4.1 provides a summary of these four types of organisation.

Characteristics	Power oriented	Role oriented	Achievement oriented	Support oriented
Type	Authoritarian, autocratic	Bureaucratic, large organisation	Consultative	Participative, listening
Values	Tradition, legitimacy, legality, honour	Legitimacy, structure, rationality, justice	Professionalism, productivity, competence, knowledge, innovation	Empathy, openness, co-operation, responsiveness, love
Focus	Focus on size, wealth, power	Focus on the role, not the individual	Focus on the achievement of a common task	Focus on the support of individuals to grow and learn
Character	Aggressive, ruthless, survival of the fittest, competition	Operate according to the rules and procedures	Tasks are assigned according to ability not role, people give loyalty and commitment to the team	Understands and operates according to the needs of the customer, nurtures individuals through development
Social control	By hierarchy and power – 'obey instructions'	By hierarchy and the rule book	By self-motivation, degree of effectiveness in terms of the organisation's goals	By self-motivation; by agreed values to serve the customer with genuine warmth
Change	Through factional struggles and positions of power	Stability valued, change resisted	Through agreed analysis of organisational needs	By continual listening, reviewing and adaptation
People who do well	Those who understand power structures, want status, wealth or power and get things done	Those who carry out their role effectively and 'keep their noses clean'	Those who are highly competent, welcome change and are high achievers	Those who care and help other individuals and departments to grow and develop
Reward system	Gives wealth, status and power – an external system of reward	Gives status and position – an external system of reward	Gives recognition, new challenges – an internal system of reward	Gives value for caring and supporting staff – an internal system of reward
Meaning of work	Work is done by low-power people to serve needs of the high-power people	Work is done to fulfil role	Work is done to complete tasks and achieve goals	Work is done to maintain the front line and develop individual potential
Customer orientation	Meeting needs of the top management can be focused only on their needs or the customers' or both as instructed	Meeting the needs of the organisation is seen as more important than the customers' needs	Offers or sells something new or better	Asks 'what can we do for you?'

TABLE 4.1: *Characteristics of organisations*

The next activity looks at the strengths and weaknesses of these different cultures.

SAT:
allow 15 mins

Managing tasks and solving problems ✓

ACTIVITY 12

Consider how the information given in table 4.1 relates to an organisation you know well. This might be the place where you do a part-time job, your work experience placement, your college or a voluntary organisation in which you are involved.

1. Which type of culture most accurately describes your chosen organisation?

2. What evidence do you have for making this judgement?

3. What, according to table 4.1, are the typical strengths and weaknesses of this type of organisation culture?

4. How far are these strengths and weaknesses reflected in the organisation you are considering?

Commentary...

It is clear that Harrison holds the view that achievement and support-oriented organisations are most likely to be successful in the context of modern environmental conditions. However, there are strengths and weaknesses associated with all four types of organisations, as shown in table 4.2.

Type	Strengths	Weaknesses
Power	Able to make decisions relatively quickly, because they are made at the top with little consultation	The organisation is unlikely to be open to ideas and initiatives that come from anywhere other than senior management.
Role	Likes working with rules and procedures and it is likely to be successful during times of stability	The culture of the organisation works against co-operation and communication and this means that the organisation will be slow to identify changes in customers' requirements.
Achievement	Encourages co-operation, communication and team work	It is not always sensitive to needs of individual customers and it can be slow to make important decisions.
Support	Is particularly good at identifying customers' needs	It frequently fails to pay attention to the systems that can meet these needs. People are more important to this type of organisation than achieving the task.

TABLE 4.2: *Strengths and weaknesses of different types of organisations.*

Harrison observed that the achievement and support types of organisation have become increasingly common and successful in the previous two decades. The challenge for those who want to move towards 'achievement' and 'support' oriented cultures is how to overcome the drawbacks of those cultures.

Managers can do this by planning strategies that include developing approaches and systems that keep the organisation close to the customer, designing vertical and horizontal communication channels that enable information to flow freely and quickly around the organisation and by ensuring that decision-making processes are appropriate and effective.

Analysing strengths and opportunities

Although it is not strictly a part of the planning process, awareness of strengths and opportunities in the external environment as well as within the organisation itself is the real starting point for planning change. It is important for managers to take a preliminary look at possible future opportunities and to see them clearly and completely. They must know where the organisation stands in the light of its strengths and weaknesses, understand what problems they face and how they might solve these. Setting realistic objectives depends on this awareness.

Thus, introducing appropriate change inevitably forces businesses to ask themselves a number of challenging questions:

- What business are we in?

- Where do we want to be in the medium- and long-term future?

Answering these questions must involve the organisation in an honest analysis of:

- the purpose of the business and what it is setting out to achieve

- its own strengths and weaknesses

- its competitors and their strengths and weaknesses

- the potential threats and possible opportunities presented by the marketplace and the wider external environment.

Although this type of analysis may be initiated by senior managers, the breadth of thinking it entails is important for all employees and managers at all levels. Determining the strengths, weaknesses, opportunities and threats of every aspect of the business should always be a starting point when planning for the future.

A **SWOT** (strengths, weaknesses, opportunities, threats) analysis can be used at any stage of the life of an organisation and can be applied to any problem. It is a particularly valuable exercise when planning because it gives managers a fundamental understanding of the purpose of their business.

A SWOT analysis is usually set out within the four sections of a window; the positive points being written on the left-hand side and the negative ones on the right. As you can see from figure 4.4, the SWOT framework will generate a great deal of useful information – and may produce some surprises.

ANALYSING STRENGTHS
AND OPPORTUNITIES

Strengths	Weaknesses
What does the organisation do (well)?	What do customers complain about?
What skills does it have?	Are there any skills gaps?
What resources does it have?	What about staff morale?
Does it have a strong financial base?	Which resources does the organisation lack?
Does it have strong client/patient base?	Is any equipment old or outdated?
Does it have a good reputation?	Is there sufficient demand for products?
Opportunities	**Threats**
Which national or local trends or changes may open up a demand for a new or existing product or service?	Which trends or changes may reduce demand for the organisation's products?
Can the organisation present the existing product or service in a new market?	Which other providers might compete for contracts or customers?
Which new products or services could be made or provided?	Is the business threatened by technological changes?
Does new technology offer the business increased opportunities?	Is the business threatened by legislation or government restrictions?

FIGURE 4.4: *SWOT analysis.*

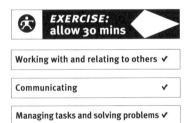

EXERCISE:
allow 30 mins

Working with and relating to others ✔

Communicating ✔

Managing tasks and solving problems ✔

ACTIVITY 13

Working in a small group, study the article about the drugs group Fisons given in Resource 2 (at the back of this workbook). Then construct a SWOT analysis for that organisation, based on the information given in the article.

Strengths	Weaknesses
Opportunities	**Threats**

Commentary...

Do not worry if the results of your SWOT analysis does not match exactly the one given in figure 4.5. It would be rare for two people's perceptions of the same situation to be exactly the same. The skill is in considering something from all the different angles and then using this as a bridge to help in determining future plans.

Strengths	Weaknesses
The value of its respiratory medicine delivery technology	Over reliance on marketing other people's medicines
It has a sound future as an independent company.	Absence of new medicines to replace the ageing anti-asthma drugs has fuelled speculation that Fisons has no future on its own.
It has not sold the whole of its R&D arm. The unit dealing with asthma and other breathing difficulties is still within the company.	
Opportunities	**Threats**
Its lead in respiratory medicines gives it a flying start in the emergent new field of drugs for related illnesses.	The hostile £1.7 billion bid from Rhone Poulenc Rorer.
It would agree to an offer that would value properly the company's respiratory technology.	The asthma scare which has led to a low bid from RPR.

FIGURE 4.5: *SWOT analysis for Fisons.*

When managers conduct a SWOT analysis they have to make sure that they:

- analyse the current position honestly

- base their analysis on hard data rather than subjective impressions

- find evidence to back up any points derived from subjective analysis

- identify areas of action indicated by the analysis

- identify areas where the organisation may need to be protected from competition or developed.

Once the factors which determine the position of a business have been identified, the next step is to reinforce or strengthen the positive aspects and to rectify the negative ones.

**ANALYSING STRENGTHS
AND OPPORTUNITIES**

Plans should:

- build on the identified strengths

- turn the weaknesses into strengths

- make the most of opportunities

- plan a way around the threats.

ANALYSING YOUR OWN STRENGTHS AND WEAKNESSES

The readiness to initiate and manage personal as well as organisational change is a key part of an effective manager's role. SWOT analysis can be a useful tool for building a picture of personal strengths and weaknesses in relation to long- or short-term career and personal goals.

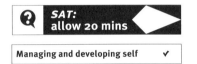

SAT:
allow 20 mins

Managing and developing self ✓

ACTIVITY 14

Write down a goal that is important to you. Now do a SWOT analysis that describes your own position in relation to it, making notes in the box below.

Strengths	Weaknesses
Opportunities	**Threats**

The picture that you build up will help you to put together an action plan for change.

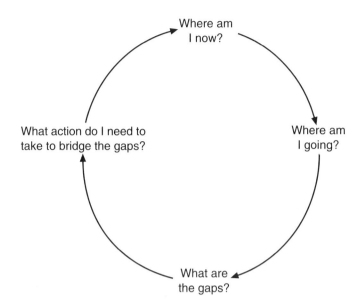

FIGURE 4.6: *A personal action plan.*

It is interesting to realise that almost everything that applies to organisations applies equally to you as an individual. Indeed, an organisation's capacity to plan and manage change depends to a great extent on the ability of the individuals within it to adapt to new ways of working and to introduce innovative ideas.

Building a risk window

SWOT analyses often produce unexpected findings that can have radical implications for the future of the business. Managers may often find that possibilities exist for expanding into new areas of the market. Expansion can be achieved by one, or a combination, of the following strategies:

- providing more of the same service in the existing market

- offering the same service in a new market

- offering a new service in the existing market

- offering a new service in a new market.

However, there is always a risk associated with expanding or changing priorities. In general terms, the further businesses move away from what they are already doing, the greater the risk. Figure 4.7 shows a convenient way of showing this – a 'risk window'.

BUILDING A RISK WINDOW

	Same service	New service
Same market	*Low risk –* hope to expand by offering a more efficient, better quality service	*Medium risk–* develop a related or completely new service
New market	*Medium risk –* expand by adapting current service to satisfy the needs of a new market	*High risk –* develop a new service and find a new market in which to sell it.

FIGURE 4.7: *A risk window.*

NHS TRUST

For several years, a human resources department has been providing management development training for a number of different functions and teams within an NHS Trust. Having done a SWOT analysis to establish how it can expand and develop, the human resource team produced a number of ideas:

- to promote management development training more effectively within the Trust to increase the take up rate for the service

- to offer a career development consultancy service within the Trust

- to offer management development training to local authority social services, voluntary organisations and private residential homes

- to develop a new range of services, including information technology training, creativity development, NVQ assessor training and offer all these both within the Trust and on the open market.

SAT:
allow 5 mins

Managing tasks and solving problems ✓

ACTIVITY 15

Draw a risk window for the above HR department, using the grid below.

	Same service	New Service
Same market		
New market		

Commentary...

Figure 4.8 shows what your risk window should look like.

	Same service	New service
Same market	Promote management development training more effectively within the Trust to increase the take up rate for the service.	Offer a career development consultancy service within the Trust.
New market	Offer management development training to local authority social services, voluntary organisations and private residential homes.	Develop a new range of services, including information technology training, creativity development, NVQ assessor training and offer all these both within the Trust and on the open market.

FIGURE 4.8: *Risk window for a NHS Trust human resources department.*

SWOT analysis tells you where you are, and the risk window tells you about where you might want to be, but it is the strategic and operational plans that answer the all-important question – 'How do we get there from here?'

In section 2, we explore the techniques that managers use when they make their planning decisions.

summary

▶ The plans that a business makes are influenced by a range of forces in the external environment. Those forces are continually changing, and the speed at which they change is increasing all the time.

▶ The six main environmental influences on the structure and the growth of any organisation are: politics, economics, social trends, technology, the law and the environment (PESTLE).

▶ The attitudes and actions of our political leaders and legislators affect virtually every aspect of life and every business organisation. Changes and developments in the national and international economy have a significant impact on both business organisations and public service organisations.

▶ When planning, managers must always take into account social structure, and the attitudes, desires, expectations, and customs of the people who live in the social environment.

▶ To survive in a changing world, every business must keep abreast of the technology applicable to its products and services and to its methods of operation.

▶ The legal environment is a complex mix of laws, regulations and government agencies and their actions, which affect all kinds of organisations to varying degrees.

▶ Recent years have witnessed the emergence of green consumerism as the business response to growing environmental awareness.

▶ Managers need to understand the predominant organisational culture and how this can act as a constraint on organisational plans. Experience has shown that there is a greater likelihood of achieving change if efforts are directed at culture rather than by using structural or procedural methods alone.

Decision Making

What decision making involves

Objectives

After participating in this session, you should be able to:

▶ explain the importance of effective decision making in a business context

▶ differentiate between different types of decision

▶ identify the right decision style to use in a given situation

▶ state the key steps in decision making

▶ explore the implications of an unstructured approach to decision making.

In working through this session, you will practise the following BTEC common skills:

Managing and developing self	✔
Working with and relating to others	✔
Communicating	✔
Managing tasks and solving problems	✔
Applying numeracy	
Applying technology	
Applying design and creativity	

The importance of decision making

The first section of this workbook looked at how the development of an organisation and the quality of the work it produces revolve around a core of decision making. The process is a central one because it links so closely to planning:

- Making decisions is a means by which organisations select their goals and objectives.

- Making decisions is how people move their work on to achieve their objectives and tasks.

- The way in which decisions are made can determine the extent to which people are committed to the content of a plan.

So, decision making is a vital management task. An organisation's well-being, effectiveness and very survival depend almost entirely on the quality of its decision-making processes.

Many writers have noted how closely planning and decision making are bound together. For example, Snyder and Glueck defined planning as:

... those activities which are concerned specifically with determining in advance what actions and/or human and physical resources are required to reach a goal. It includes identifying alternatives, analysing each one, and selecting the best ones.

Snyder, N. and Glueck, N.F., 1980, 'How managers plan – the analysis of managerial activities, in *Long Range Planning*, vol. XIII, February, pp. 70–6.

This definition could just as easily have been applied to decision making.

In fact the term 'decision making' has sometimes been used as a virtual synonym for planning. Assuming that a 'decision' involves a commitment to future action, it is argued that every decision must therefore constitute a plan or part of a plan. It does not matter whether that decision involves an activity that will take place in ten minutes' or in two years' time.

Another view of planning purports that it is not so much concerned with the making of individual decisions but of integrating different ones. In his book *The Rise and Fall of Strategic Planning,* Henry Mintzberg (Prentice Hall, 1994) states that 'planning is a formalised procedure to produce an articulated result, in the form of an integrated system of decisions'.

'Formalisation' here refers to analysing and rationalising the processes by which decisions are made and integrated into organisations. In this part of the workbook, we set out to do just this - to make the different phases and elements of decision making explicit, so that it is possible to see more clearly:

- how the process relates to planning

- how it can be improved by applying certain techniques

- how organisations depend for their success on effective decision making.

But what exactly is a decision?

ACTIVITY 1

This activity will help to sharpen your awareness of the vast range of different types of decision that you make in the course of a normal day. Take ten minutes to write a list of the decisions you made yesterday. Don't stop to consider how they were made or how important they were, just write everything down.

You may like to divide these decisions under different sub-headings such as 'at home', 'leisure time' or 'study time'.

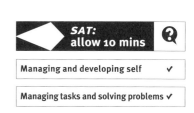

SAT:
allow 10 mins

Managing and developing self ✓

Managing tasks and solving problems ✓

Commentary...

It's impossible to give you feedback on what you have written, but compare your list with one made by another BTEC student.

At home:

- Whether or not to go for a run before breakfast
- What to have for breakfast
- Whether to travel on the bus or walk
- How to fit household chores in with the day's activities
- In which order to tackle chores
- Mother is ill – how to cope with taking younger children to school
- Arrangements for a family birthday party

In a union meeting:

- Whether or not to wait for latecomers
- Order of the agenda
- Who will take notes?
- How to move current campaigns forward
- How to tackle some of the issues which require further research and or consultation
- Activities for the next month
- The composition of subgroups
- Allocating tasks and agreeing roles
- Tickets for the monthly disco are not selling well – how are we going to deal with this?
- We want to introduce a college newsletter. What do people want? What would interest them?
- When and where shall we meet next time?

During study time:

- When and where to do private study
- Which piece of work should take priority
- How to tackle a piece of work
- Suddenly realise that a project deadline is approaching faster than expected – how to revise timetable to complete it on time

- Where to find required resources
- How to deal with interruptions

With friends:

- How to spend leisure time in the evening
- Who to invite to come along
- What time to arrive/go home
- The bus company has revised its timetable so that the last bus home from town is far too early. How are we going to get home today and in the future?

The more you think about it, the more you realise that you are taking decisions, or that decisions are being made for you, virtually all the time. The important point for organisations is that they should be aware of the times when they are making decisions, and that they should not just happen by default.

An exercise like the previous activity is useful for the following reasons:

- It starts to make you analyse how you are **dividing your time** up between the different areas of your life. What are your priorities?

- It starts to make you analyse **how you make decisions**. Do you stand back and make a rational, considered choice or do they just happen?

- It starts to make you analyse **your approach** to the decisions which have an impact on the way you spend your time. Do you make the key decisions of the day in a planned and rational way beforehand – or do you make each decision as it comes along?

You can begin to see how a more formal approach to making decisions can help us to allocate our time more efficiently and to get through the work and leisure activities that we want to accomplish during a particular day or week.

In the same way, organisations find it valuable to adopt decision-making processes that help them first to select appropriate goals and objectives and then to choose the most appropriate ways of achieving these. But the art of good decision making is a very complex process, and it is not easy to ensure that all managers have the necessary skills. These include a whole range of technical, personal and interpersonal skills like the ability to analyse, logical thinking, self-awareness, sensitivity to others, assertiveness and communication.

LEVELS OF DECISION MAKING

In business, decisions occur constantly and simultaneously at a number of levels. These correspond to the planning levels discussed in the first part of the workbook.

At the **strategic level,** decisions have to be made about, for example:

- the overall purpose and direction of the organisation

- how systems and structures need to be changed or developed

- long-term performance or production targets

- how to respond to competitor activity.

At the **operational level,** managers make decisions about, for example:

- how the department or function can contribute to long-term organisational goals

- the allocation of tasks and resources to achieve desired objectives

- scheduling of staff

- how to solve problems or improve work processes.

At the **individual level,** decisions have to made about, for example:

- how people can best contribute to achieving objectives

- which resources they need

- how much support or training they need.

ACTIVITY 2

Categorise the levels of the following decisions:

(a) Whether or not to send someone on a computer skills training course

(b) Whether or not to merge with another company

(c) How to develop team communication systems

(d) How to respond to a competitor's strategy

(e) How to reduce waste in the production department

Commentary...

You should have noted that (a) is a decision at the individual level, (b) and (d) are at the strategic level, and (c) and (e) are at the operational level.

As we saw in the first part of the workbook, planning or decision making should ideally be both a top-down and bottom-up process because people will not, in general, be committed to a plan or decision which affects them but in which they have not participated.

This workbook aims to take you through some of the approaches organisations and people use to make decisions and to help you to judge their usefulness in various circumstances.

Types of decision

It is valuable to identify the types of decision that are made in a business context. Knowing what type of decision they are dealing with helps managers to decide at what level, how and when the decision should be made.

GROUPING ACCORDING TO RESPONSIBILITY

A common way of classifying decisions is to group them in a way that indicates who might have responsibility for making them. Thus we have decisions which are routine, urgent, problematic or consultative.

Routine

These are ordinary decisions on a wide range of issues, such as when the next meeting should be held, which problem to tackle first, how to deal with standard customer complaints and so on. It often saves time if these decisions are left to a manager or leader.

Urgent

Some problems occur rapidly and may have serious consequences if not dealt with immediately. These include unforeseen events such as the sudden illness of an employee, awareness of a safety hazard or the breakdown of equipment. Again a manager will often deal with these personally and explain or justify them later.

Problematic

These sorts of decisions must be taken when a difficulty has emerged and there is no obvious solution. Examples could be a sales decrease for no obvious reason or having to cope with a new product from a competitor. It can be useful for a management team or a cross functional subgroup to focus on these; experts from outside the team may be called in to give advice.

Consultative

Sometimes it is important to involve others because they will be affected by the results of the decision. This may mean including a whole department or team in the decision-making process or again, consulting other people from outside. Decisions of this sort could include introducing new systems, changing structures or procedures and bringing in new technology.

ACTIVITY 3

In activity 1 in this session, you listed some of the decisions you made yesterday. Categorise these decisions into routine, urgent, problematic and consultative decisions.

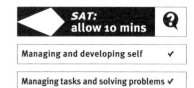

SAT:
allow 10 mins

Managing and developing self ✓

Managing tasks and solving problems ✓

Commentary...

As a comparison with the decisions you have identified, here are some examples taken from the list we provided earlier in the section.

Routine:

- What to have for breakfast

- Whether or not to wait for latecomers

- When and where to do private study

Urgent:

- Mother is ill - how to cope with the crisis of taking younger children to school

- Suddenly realise that a project deadline is approaching faster than expected – how to revise timetable to complete it on time.

Problematic:

- How to fit household chores in with the day's activities

- How to move current campaigns forward

- Tickets for the monthly disco are not selling well – how are we going to deal with this?

- How to deal with interruptions

- The bus company has revised its timetable so that the last bus home from town is far too early. How are we going to get home today and in the future?

Consultative:

- Arrangements for a family birthday party

- We want to introduce a college newsletter. What do people want? What would interest them?

- Allocating tasks and agreeing roles

- What time to arrive/go home

This classification is largely a matter of personal choice and will depend on the particular circumstances of the individual decision. Nevertheless, even a subjective interpretation will help decision makers to select an appropriate way of tackling a particular decision.

GROUPING ACCORDING TO CHARACTER

Another method by which we can categorise decisions is one mentioned in *Making Management Decisions* by Cook and Slack (2nd edn, 1991, Prentice Hall). This method identifies three 'general dimensions' of a decision.

First, is the decision **strategic** or **operational?** Here 'strategic' decisions are taken to mean ones that relate the organisation to its environment and involve a large part of the organisation. Operational decisions are those that relate to departments or functions.

- 'Which overseas markets to enter' would be a strategic decision.

- 'How to organise the production schedule' would be an operational decision.

Second, is the decision **structured** or **unstructured?** Some decisions are clear, well-defined and unambiguous while others are indistinct and difficult to tackle. Structured decisions are easier to make because the decision maker knows the extent of the decision and the options are clear. With unstructured decisions, however, the options are not immediately apparent because the decision has not occurred in these circumstances before.

- 'Shall we go for a red border or a blue one?' is a structured decision.

- 'Pilfering is a problem that has never occurred on this scale before. What are we going to do?' is an unstructured decision.

Third, is the decision **dependent** or **independent?** The degree of dependency of a decision can be measured on two scales. The first scale represents the influence of past and future decisions and the second one represents the degree of influence across other areas of the organisation. Some decisions are relatively limited in their effect on the rest of the organisation, others have wide-ranging consequences.

- 'How are we going to tackle staff appraisals this year?' is a dependent decision.

- 'The next item on the agenda is to organise the team duty rota' is an independent decision.

The writers point out that, as a general rule, 'strategic decisions tend to be unstructured and dependent, whereas operational decisions tend to be structured and independent'.

ACTIVITY 4

Read the following scenarios.

Sales of the journal have been decreasing slowly but surely over the past year. Feedback from readers seems to indicate that there is some dissatisfaction with both the nature and the range of articles and they would like to see more advertisements for jobs. I am not sure whether to go for a complete rethink of the whole journal - a course of action which would be very costly - or just to inject subtle changes here and there where it can be done without great expense. Then again it could be that we need a new design or maybe some fresh writers would improve matters.

Editor of a professional journal

I have to decide which order to process first this week and this is somewhat difficult because I have two customers who appear to have submitted identical orders. However this does not mean that they have to be treated equally. My policy is to try to find out if one of them was placed late or asked for early and whether either of them has come from a notoriously slow payer. I also check whether one firm may be about to place another big order if this one progresses satisfactorily.

Production manager in a shirt factory

Which of the decisions described in the above scenarios is dependent or independent and which is structured or unstructured? Give reasons for your answer.

Commentary...

The editor's decision is unstructured and dependent. It is not clear who is responsible for making the decision and neither the problem nor the options are well defined. This decision is not likely to have occurred before in precisely these circumstances. Whatever the outcome of the decision, it will have a considerable effect on the future of the organisation, and will have ramifications for staff in all departments.

The production manager's decision is structured and independent. The decision maker knows the options that are available and the decision is not an unfamiliar one. He or she has already thought through the evaluation criteria and seems to have a clearly defined procedure to follow in order to make a choice. Furthermore, the decision will have a limited effect on the rest of the organisation.

Styles of decision making

A key decision-making skill is in knowing who should take the decision and when and how it should be taken. Traditionally, managers or leaders have assumed the authority to take decisions alone and to pass them down the line for implementation. Nowadays, successful organisations often try to ensure that problematic or consultative decisions are made by appropriate work groups or management teams. Decisions made by the wrong people at the wrong time can have disastrous implications when they are implemented.

A valuable way of reaching a better understanding of the different approaches to decision making is to locate them on a continuum. This relates closely to the three management styles looked at in session 1 of section 1 of this workbook.

RECALL:
allow 10 mins

Name the three management styles mentioned in section 1, session 1 and explain what each one means.

The chart in table 1.1 is based on research by Tannbaum and Schmidt and was reported in the *Harvard Business Review* in 1973. At one end of the continuum, the autocratic manager makes all the choices and merely tells subordinates what he or she has decided. At the other end lies the participative approach where responsibility for decision making is shared between members of a whole team. In between the two extremes lie a range of decision-making processes in which the team leader or subgroup 'sells' the decision to the rest of the team. Their input can then be anything from a virtual rubber stamp to a wide-ranging discussion which will determine whether or not the team will support the proposal. The approaches at the top of table 1.1 are **autocratic,** the ones in the middle are **consultative** and the ones at the bottom are **participative**.

Approach
The manager makes decisions which are accepted by the group.
The manager sells the decision to the group before gaining acceptance.
The manager presents the decision but responds to questions from the group.
The manager presents a tentative decision subject to change on the basis of group inputs.
The manager presents a problem, gets input from the group and then decides.
The manager defines the limits within which the group should make the decision.
The manager and the group make the decision jointly.

TABLE 1.1: *Different approaches to decision making*

As you will probably have gathered by now, this workbook seeks to counterbalance the historical predominance of the top-down or autocratic attitude to making decisions. Although we are generally concerned with promoting participative procedures, it is important to remember that, in decision making, both perspectives have their place. A major component of the art of management is to be able to choose the appropriate style for a particular task. The right approach for a given situation might be democratic and participative or autocratic and directive, or indeed any point on the spectrum in between.

The following case study serves to highlight some of the problems which may occur if the wrong style is selected in the decision-making process.

CHRIS BAXTER

After 20 years of loyal service, Chris Baxter was eventually promoted to purchasing manager in a large engineering firm in the North East of England. Chris had made slow but sure progress thanks to persistence, attention to detail and a willingness to do whatever it took to unravel complex financial muddles. Chris was less skilled in dealing with people, however, and was generally considered to be rather stand-offish, formal and awkward when dealing with colleagues.

Nevertheless, Chris was delighted at the promotion and without the slightest hesitation started planning the complete reorganisation of the department. At last, there was a chance to get things done the right way, after years of having to put up with the 'ineffective and frustrating' systems imposed by the former departmental manager. Chris spent a whole week planning in great detail and the first anyone knew about the proposed changes was a four-page memo which was sent to all group managers. This set out, in great detail, instructions for the new purchasing procedures.

This initiative set off a chain reaction resulting in an immediate drop in performance in the department and a noticeable lowering of staff morale. In less than a week, the personnel department received several enquiries about transfers and two requests for early retirement. Meanwhile Chris's plans for change were overtaken by the board's success in merging with another company in the Midlands. The initiative for change had to be put on hold while the task of bringing the two companies together could be completed.

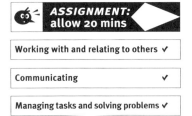

Working with and relating to others ✔

Communicating   ✔

Managing tasks and solving problems ✔

ACTIVITY 5

Reflect on the issues which have emerged from the case study:

- Give reasons why you think that Chris chose to adopt a 'top-down' approach to decision making.

- Explain why the staff reacted in the way they did.

- Describe how Chris might have otherwise gone about the task of deciding what had to be done to improve performance in the department.

Write your report on a separate sheet of paper. Use the box below to note your main ideas.

Key steps in decision making

The army first discovered that leaders using a systematic approach to making decisions usually have more success than those who fail to impose methodical processes. During the Second World War soldiers developed disciplined thought habits that used their mental energy to the best advantage. Since that time managers in the commercial world have adopted these techniques for structuring their thinking, solving problems and making better decisions.

Figure 1.1 illustrates how decision making forms part of the broader process of problem solving.

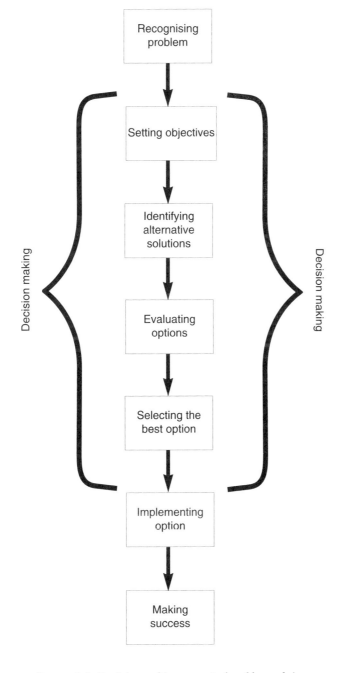

FIGURE 1.1: *Decision making as part of problem solving.*

Before moving on to examine the main steps in the systematic decision-making process it is worth exploring briefly the differences between 'decision making' and 'problem solving'. Although the two activities are very closely connected, and are often taken by management writers to mean the same thing, the terms are not interchangeable. Decisions may be made in the absence of an identifiable problem, and problem solving often involves other elements as well as decision making.

In this workbook we are concerned with the steps identified as the systematic decision-making process:

Setting objectives

Here, decision makers must define the purpose of the decision and consider what outcomes or objectives it will achieve. In some cases, these objectives will have to relate to the overall objectives of the organisation.

Identifying alternative solutions

It is important to gather all possible options; some are obvious, others have to be logically deduced while others require a more creative approach. Sessions 3 and 4 deal with this phase of the process.

Evaluating options

This step involves determining the extent to which the decision options meets the decision objectives defined earlier. Here, the costs and benefits of each option may be spelt out in some detail, sometimes using a mathematical model. We look at this step in session 4.

Selecting the best option

After evaluation, the 'best' option is selected using any one of a number of techniques or approaches that we discuss in session 4 of this part of the workbook.

Most managers feel they know the process outlined here yet many of them are still poor decision makers. Here is what some of them have said about the process of making decisions.

> **The trouble is that sometimes I don't think things through enough before jumping in with both feet.**
>
> Rose, manager of a residential home

I get so worried about important decisions that I can't actually make a decision at all!

Andy, operations manager in a communications company

They say the key to decision making is creativity, but I'm not at all creative so my decisions must be poor.

Teresa, customer services manager

Problems like these can cause frustration, waste money, reduce morale, weaken commitment and bring about poor performance. Some managers simply lack confidence, but managers sometimes lack competence in decision making. The most common reasons for poor decision making are:

- failure to identify objectives

- taking a narrow perspective

- lack of discipline

- inadequate evaluation

- indecision.

Failure to identify objectives

Neglecting to define the purpose of the decision means that the whole process lacks focus. It is difficult to arrive at a result when you don't know what you want the outcome to be.

Taking a narrow perspective

The most effective and appropriate options may be missed if decision makers fail to think broadly, logically and creatively about the decision in hand.

Lack of discipline

There is a risk of rushing too quickly towards a conclusion and failing to go through the steps of the process methodically.

Inadequate evaluation

A wrong decision can be made if those responsible fail to stop and evaluate each possible option with the utmost care.

Indecision

People are sometimes afraid to commit themselves finally to a firm decision. But if the decision makers understand the objectives, if they have considered all possible alternatives and the range of consequences, they should be able to take a firm stand with confidence.

Effective decision makers try to monitor the strengths and weaknesses of their own approach, so that they can continually produce better outcomes.

summary

▶ Decision making is a vital management task. An organisation's well-being, effectiveness and very survival depend almost entirely on the quality of its decision-making processes.

▶ In business, decisions occur constantly and simultaneously at strategic, operational and individual levels. These correspond to the planning levels discussed in section 1 of this workbook.

▶ A common way of classifying decisions is to group them in a way that indicates who might have responsibility for making them. Thus we have decisions which are routine, urgent, problematic or consultative.

▶ Decisions can also be classified according to whether they are strategic or operational, structured or unstructured, dependent or independent.

▶ Decision making should ideally be both a top-down and bottom-up process because people will not in general be committed to a decision which affects them but in which they have not participated.

▶ Traditionally, managers or leaders have assumed the authority to take decisions alone and to pass them down the line for implementation. Nowadays, successful organisations often try to ensure that problematic or consultative decisions are made by appropriate work groups or management teams.

▶ Although decision making and problem solving are very closely connected, the terms are not interchangeable. Decisions may be made in the absence of an identifiable problem, and problem solving often involves other elements as well as decision making.

Obtaining information for decisions

THE NEED FOR HIGH
QUALITY INFORMATION

TYPES OF INFORMATION

SOURCES OF INFORMATION

INFORMATION FLOW
AND ORGANISATIONAL
STRUCTURE

Objectives

After participating in this session, you should be able to:

▶ explain the need for high quality information for effective decision making

▶ differentiate between the types of information required by businesses

▶ identify a variety of sources of information for decision making

▶ explain how flexible decentralised structures improve information flow

▶ describe how computerised communication networks make decision making more effective.

In working through this session, you will practise the following BTEC common skills:

Managing and developing self	✔
Working with and relating to others	✔
Communicating	✔
Managing tasks and solving problems	✔
Applying numeracy	✔
Applying technology	
Applying design and creativity	✔

The need for high quality information

Before exploring the stages of decision making in detail, it is important to examine the vital role that information plays throughout the process.

Many managers speak of an **information crisis** existing within business organisations. Paradoxically, this often means too much information and, at the same time, too little. They have to cope with too much of the kind of information that swamps them with irrelevant detail and receive too little information which is accurate, timely and relevant.

To make effective decisions, it is vital that decision makers have the right information at the right time. For example, an organisation can use information to react more quickly than its competitors to a particular fact or circumstance. The business that makes the correct strategic decision first can greatly improve and strengthen its position in relation to its competitors.

Decision makers need information that is appropriate for the choices that they need to make:

- to make planning decisions, organisations need relevant information about environmental trends

- to make control decisions they need to know how current performance compares with target figures.

To be useful, information should be:

- relevant

- supplied in appropriate detail

- accurate

- complete

- timely

- effectively presented.

Relevance

Incomplete information means that decision makers have to work in the dark. Extraneous information, on the other hand, wastes time, obscures the vital facts, congests the information channels and increases administrative costs.

In one large national organisation, over 200 copies were made of a single report and sent to everyone who might be remotely affected or interested. It took a month for the report to reach the key decision maker, yet a large number of other people found themselves reading it unnecessarily. If anyone had stopped to calculate the costs of photocopying and administrative time, they would have soon realised that these were far in excess of the benefits of such a wide circulation.

Detail

People at different levels of the organisation have widely differing information requirements. At the strategic level where long-term plans and broad control decisions are made, managers require a broad sweep of information from all parts of the organisation; however the amount of detail needed is slight. Managers at the operational level, on the other hand, have a relatively narrow area of interest and need much more detail.

One consequence of new technology is that more information is available than is strictly necessary. Customer databases are one example of an area where the information asked for is often more than is required. Companies then have to invest a substantial amount of time in entering a large number of irrelevant details that they will probably never use either for making decisions or for any other purposes.

On the other hand, some information needs to be logged continuously and the cost of collecting this is justified because it affects important decisions.

Accuracy

Inaccurate information may lead to poor decision making. However, the expense of achieving a high degree of accuracy must be balanced against the expected benefits.

Inaccuracy can occur in a number of ways.

- The method of collecting data can lead to **bias**. This often happens in market research surveys where the cost-effective way of collecting data is to question shoppers in the town centre. The sample selected in this way may not, however, be representative of the population as a whole.

- Data may be **entered incorrectly** into the computerised database or manual recording system. Such mistakes can lead to costly errors in decision making.

● **Invalid assumptions** may be made when information is produced from the raw data. This may happen, for example, when financial managers apportion overheads to departments according to a generalised formula.

Note, **data** is the raw facts and figures collected by an information system from a variety of internal and external sources. Information processing can turn this data into useful **information,** on which decisions and actions can be based.

Completeness

Like accuracy, completeness can only be judged in relative terms. It would make no sense to hold up a vital decision because the information required was not yet complete. If a patient needed urgent medical treatment, it would not be advisable to wait until his or her medical records were brought right up-to-date. There generally has to be a trade-off between what is available and what is desirable.

Timing

Information is only of use if it reaches the decision maker before the decision is made! Because of the need to react quickly to change, it may therefore be better to have information that is slightly less than accurate rather than to wait for information that is more accurate but takes a long time to produce. When doing a market research survey, it is sometimes better to make do with a random sample of customers' opinions than to wait for a fully fledged piece of academic research to be carried out.

Presentation

However sound the information is, it is not useful if it comes unsorted or badly presented. Much routine information is most conveniently presented in the form of reports. These may be produced at monthly, weekly or sometimes daily intervals, and should concentrate on information essential for decision making.

Research has shown that information is most easily assimilated if it is presented in the form of tables, charts or graphs. Consider the following statement from a company's annual report:

> **Some 23 per cent of our turnover is from men's shirts with a further 14 per cent from ladies' blouses and 5 per cent from ties. The highest proportion, 58 per cent, is from dressing gowns.**

This information is comprehensible but hard to digest.

A better way to present this data in the form of a pie chart (see figure 2.1) or even as a simple list – the company's turnover can be attributed to:

- shirts – 23 per cent

- blouses – 14 per cent

- ties – 5 per cent

- dressing gowns – 58 per cent.

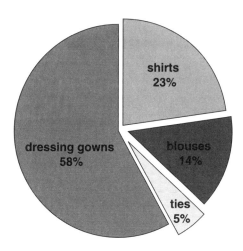

FIGURE 2.1: *Pie chart showing turnover.*

Most people would find that the simple pie chart gives the information in the form that is most immediate and powerful. The best way of conveying simple or complex information for decision making is with graphics.

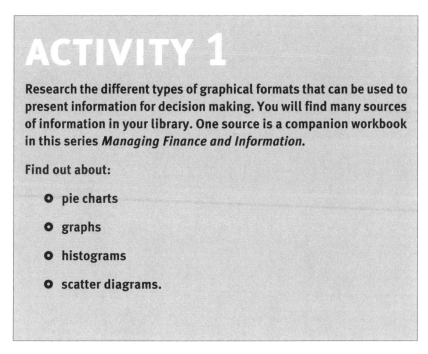

ACTIVITY 1

Research the different types of graphical formats that can be used to present information for decision making. You will find many sources of information in your library. One source is a companion workbook in this series *Managing Finance and Information.*

Find out about:

- pie charts

- graphs

- histograms

- scatter diagrams.

EXERCISE:
allow 1 hour

Managing and developing self ✔

Communicating ✔

Applying numeracy ✔

Applying design and creativity ✔

Table 2.1 shows the accident rate figures for a transport company. Present these figures using three of the above graphical formats so that trends and problems are shown at a glance.

Vehicles	1993	1994	1995
Vans	10	12	19
Pick up trucks	15	10	8
Luton vans	6	8	7
Lorries	9	13	11

TABLE 2.1: *Transport accidents by type of vehicle and year*

Does this data provide sufficient information to explain the accident problems facing the transport company, What further information would you want to know in order to make a full analysis? Identify possible weaknesses in the data you have been given in Table 2.1

Types of information

In their book *Business Information Systems and Strategies* (Prentice Hall, 1991), Carol Cashmore and Richard Lyall note that organisations need to collect, store and communicate three basic types of information:

- external information

- corporate information

- internal information.

External information is the information that flows into the organisation from the world at large. Information in this category includes:

- accumulated information about customers' requirements and preferences

- technological know-how and skills, e.g. knowledge about equipment and materials or the latest research and developments

- knowledge about the existence of distribution channels

- information about the plans and performance of competitors.

Corporate information flows from the organisation into the external environment. It includes marketing and advertising information as well as promotional information that builds the reputation and image of the business and helps to sell its products and services.

Internal information circulates inside the organisation and includes:

- the facts and figures about the organisation's performance

- information about income and expenditure

- information about managerial skills.

Traditionally, too much emphasis has been placed on the importance of internal information. Most organisations have only recently become aware of the immense value of external and corporate information for both strategic and operational decision making and planning.

TYPES OF INFORMATION

SAT:
allow 20 mins

Managing tasks and solving problems ✓

ACTIVITY 2

List the internal information a district manager of a chain of restaurants might need to know on a weekly basis.

Set out the external information a marketing manager might require when planning a medium-term marketing and communications strategy.

Describe the corporate information required by the organisation's shareholders at the end of each financial year.

Commentary...

The internal information required by the district manager from the restaurants in his or her district would include:

- sales
- profit
- staff absences
- expenditure
- health and safety problems

- customer feedback or complaints.

The marketing manager would need to know:

- information about customer preferences or requirements

- environmental information regarding social and demographic trends, fashion, lifestyle preferences and so on

- information about competitor activity

- information pointing to the most effective methods of advertising and promoting goods and services.

Shareholders would require:

- information on sales and profits, possibly broken down by district, individual location or region

- the chairperson's report on performance during the past year, including how this had been affected by factors in the external environment

- dividend declarations.

If several organisations are in competition with each other the one that has the highest quality information is in the position to make the best decisions, design winning strategies and achieve competitive advantage.

Sources of information

We have seen that information is required at several stages of the decision-making process. It is required to **identify problems** in the first place. Managers need to collect information continually from both the external environment (political, economic, social, etc.) and from inside the organisation so that they can be aware of any changes that might affect profit or performance.

Information also assists in the **identification of appropriate options** and the selection of the best solution. Managers will find it much easier to make a choice if they take the trouble to inform themselves of the initiatives that their competitors or other businesses are taking.

Finally, information is needed to **monitor the success** of the chosen solution. Information is needed to measure how well the chosen course of action is achieving the objectives set for it.

Despite the growth of information technology, it would be wrong to imagine that all information systems and sources are, or should be, computer based. To meet the needs of decision makers, information flows into an organisation from a vast number of sources. These can be categorised into three main types:

- human sources
- written or manual sources
- information technology sources.

Human sources

People are both an important source of information and a vital information processing system. As they go about their daily work they collect many items of information from customers, colleagues and shareholders. They store and process most of these in their brains, but some of it is written down in diaries or on notepads. Later on, it is retrieved and integrated with other information to aid decision making.

Written or manual sources

Most businesses still use paper records, filing cabinets, wall charts and diaries. The 'paperless office' was one of the predictions of the early 1980s that has, as yet, failed to materialise. Indeed, there are circumstances in which people have found that the paper-based alternative is faster, more flexible and easier to use. For example, many people still prefer to note appointments in a diary rather than on a computer database.

Information technology sources

These include databases, CD-ROM, and the Internet. **Databases** store data in a way that allows information to be drawn from them in a range of different ways and formats in order to answer a range of management questions.

CD-ROMs (compact disk, read only memory) look like CDs purchased from music stores, and perform the same function: storing digital information. Vast amounts of information can be stored on CD-ROM, e.g. annual reports and company information, newspapers, dictionaries and textbooks.

The **Internet** allows access to such a vast range of data that its usefulness is entirely governed by the sophistication of the systems that sort, filter and present information. Its use in the business community is more widely accepted in the USA, with many potential users in the UK still having reservations about security and the Internet's ability to provide information that is sufficiently specific and focused.

In the academic world, however, it has become an essential means of sharing and gaining access to information, and until recently much of the impetus for the Internet's development has come from this quarter. Now, however, companies such as Microsoft and IBM are developing systems that will eventually make the Internet the major source of information transfer.

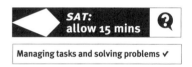

SAT:
allow 15 mins

Managing tasks and solving problems ✔

ACTIVITY 3

Imagine that you work for a tile manufacturing company that keeps all its information about customers and potential customers on a database.

- ● What items of information would you need to store on the database?

- ● Where could you obtain this information?

- ● How would this information help you to make decisions?

Commentary...

Essential information you would need to store would include:

- customer name
- customer address
- customer telephone number.

Additional information that would be valuable for marketing would include details about individual customer's socio-economic group and lifestyle or details on corporate customers' business operations and development.

There are three major methods for obtaining information about customers and potential customers:

- from sales invoices
- from the salesforce
- externally from documents like newspapers, journals and annual reports and from external databases.

You would use this information to make decisions about how to develop the organisation, to relate products to the needs of particular customer groups, to develop new products, and to plan and target promotional campaigns.

Effective business information systems are created by linking different sources of information and types of information systems, usually people, manual and computerised systems. All these sources must be appropriately balanced if an information system is to work effectively. Even in this technological age it would be wrong to discount the important role played by the human element. Expensive technology would be useless without the informal, invisible and flexible contribution of individuals who communicate with one another.

Information flow and organisational structure

Whatever form an information system takes it always breaks down into four separate elements:

- receiving information
- storing information

- using information

- communicating information.

These elements relate to the way that information flows through an organisation. Effective information flow throughout an organisation is vital to its success. But the way in which organisations are designed can create problems for decision makers by reducing the amount and quality of information available to them.

In the traditional hierarchical structure (see figure 2.2), a number of problems can arise:

- the people who are required to make and implement decisions are often based in different locations

- decisions are usually made at the top and passed downwards

- the information needed to make those decisions is passed upwards from the bottom to the top.

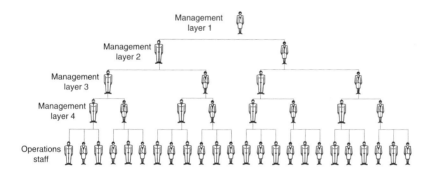

FIGURE 2.2: *A tall hierarchical structure.*

In this type of organisation, problems can arise because top managers retain all the power and do not allow lower level managers or supervisors to make decisions or influence plans. But, as you saw in section 1, decentralised 'flat' structures are becoming increasingly common as more and more organisations recognise the benefits that come from allowing autonomy and power to spread throughout the business. Having fewer tiers of management means that more decision making occurs at lower levels and that more control is devolved to operational managers.

RECALL:
allow 15 mins

Describe what is meant by a 'decentralised' organisational structure.

Decentralised structures also have their problems. Unit managers often resent the heavy direction from people at head office who are not necessarily familiar with local conditions. There may be a lack of co-operation or indeed rivalry between the different units. And people at head office may complain about uncooperative staff in the different units. In short, decentralised organisations can often become stultified by red tape and internal politics.

NETWORK STRUCTURES

Business unit networks have evolved as a response to difficulties such as these. In a network structure, the organisation is broken down into many business units which are then linked to form a corporate network.

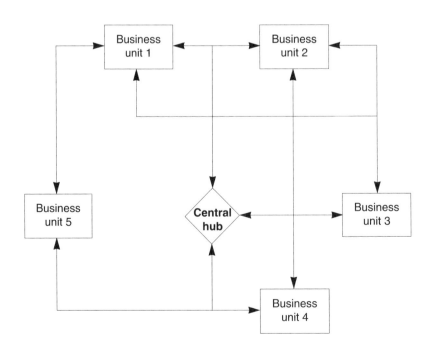

FIGURE 2.3: *A network structure.*

As in the conventional decentralised structure, strategic plans are made and resources are allocated at the corporate centre. However, because the units are linked to each other as well as to the centre, the problems of units acting in their own interests and an overall lack of strategic co-ordination are overcome. The role of head office is no longer to supervise and monitor the units but to hold them together, to support them and to co-ordinate their efforts. Olivetti has used this approach effectively and now consists of over two hundred separate firms which are linked together through a flexible network.

Such structural flexibility also promotes problem solving through team or task force action. This approach often brings small groups of people together from different functions or units to solve a particular problem or to implement a project. When the job is done the team is dispersed and other teams come together for different tasks.

The following case study shows how BP increased its effectiveness by introducing a flatter, less centralised structure and by using the team approach to problem solving.

BRITISH PETROLEUM

Early in 1990 a massive programme of change was initiated at BP by its chairman Robert Horton. His aim was to make BP the most successful oil company of the 1990s. Some changes, such as the creation of an updated logo, were relatively simple and painless. Others, involving major changes in working methods and relationships, were not. The aim, as far as the changes in the organisation structure were concerned, was to make BP as agile as a small company – not an easy task with 120,000 employees. Studies the previous year had found that many employees thought that the organisation was too bureaucratic. This view was not confined to office staff: employees on the oil rigs complained that a newly introduced safety programme entailed supervisors spending more time at a desk doing paperwork rather than outside supervising. In addition, no decision could be made on a rig without first telephoning for permission. This often entailed a two- or three-hour wait for a answer.

The hierarchies which strangled decision making had to go. Thus whole layers of management were stripped out and 27 committees were abolished. In their place, teams were created to carry out specific tasks. When the tasks were completed, the teams were disbanded. Networking was to be the 'glue' which would hold the organisation together. This would mean the creation of a good information system which would allow and encourage individuals to talk to their peers and to their bosses and subordinates. Part of this was achieved by technology and the rest by a change in attitude.

Source: Carol Cashmore and Richard Lyall, 1991,
Business Information Systems and Strategies, Prentice Hall

INFORMATION SYSTEMS FOR NETWORK STRUCTURES

Information systems reflect closely the organisation structure, and both arise as a result of the strategy chosen by the organisation in question. Network structures must be supported by a matrix of information channels that link the different units to each other and to head office. Effective decision making demands that information must be available to anyone who needs it as soon as data is collected. In many respects, network business structures have only been made possible by recent developments in telecommunication and computer technology.

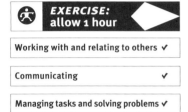

Working with and relating to others ✔

Communicating ✔

Managing tasks and solving problems ✔

ACTIVITY 4

In small groups, conduct some research into organisational communications networks. Find out what the following terms mean, drawing diagrams to illustrate the networks as appropriate:

- **LAN**

- **WAN**

- **PABX**

- **EDI**

List some of the benefits to decision makers in business organisations of using flexible computerised communication networks.

List some of the disadvantages of using flexible computerised communication networks.

Commentary...

Once you have completed your research, read the material
below and check whether you understand the main points.

A **local area network (LAN)** links PCs to a mainframe or
minicomputer over a limited geographical area. The PCs are
connected to a facility via a server that provides and regulates access
to the facility.

There are two main types of LANs: those that allow PCs to draw
information from a central database but do not let them communicate
with each other and those that do permit communication between
individual PCs. Recently more and more LANs are being set up that
consist only of a group of PCs, rather than a mainframe or
minicomputer and a number of terminals. However, some
organisations are finding that the power and flexibility of this
approach is sometimes offset by high costs and loss of security.

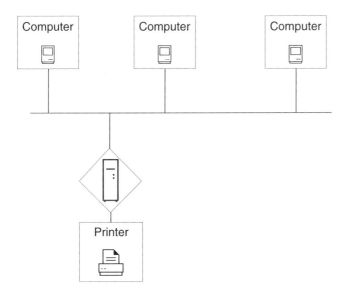

FIGURE 2.4: *A local area network.*

When LANs are connected via public or private telecommunications
networks they form **wide area networks (WANS)**. WANs connect
computers in different locations, perhaps in different parts of the
world. They may link the different sites or units of one organisation
in a large city or in one country. They may even use satellites to link
companies internationally.

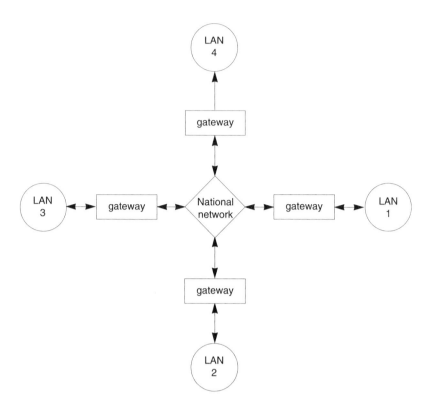

FIGURE 2.5: *A wide area network linking four LANs.*

IBM's NETWORK

In 1987, IBM set up a network which allows employees all over the world to communicate with each other. The network satisfies the IBM five-point 'anys rule':

1.   **any** employee

2.   at **any** IBM location

3.   should be able to go to **any** terminal

4.   and log on to **any** IBM application

5.   running in **any** IBM computer centre.

A **PABX (private automatic branch telephone exchange)** is used to route data and information around an organisation. PABXs at different sites can also be linked to provide WANs. PABXs were originally designed for telephone calls but can also deal with information from a PC. The advantage of the system is that costs and disruption are reduced because the telephone wiring is already in place.

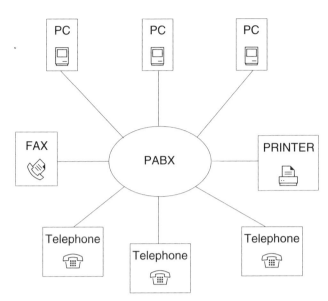

FIGURE 2.6: *A PABX LAN.*

Electronic data interchange (EDI) allows the computer systems in different companies, particularly those that have a close relationship, to link directly with each other. For example, a computer in one business, programmed with details of stock levels and reordering levels, will automatically send purchase orders to the supplier's computer as and when these are required.

RENAULT

Renault introduced a new data interchange system (a WAN) in 1987 which links the 300 UK Renault dealers with the company's factories in France. The equipment consists of a PC with a modem link to British Telecom's packet switching data transmission service. From BT, the dealers are connected through the French telephone system to Renault's mainframe computer situated in Paris where production schedules are drawn up. Apart from speeding up the ordering process, this system has the advantage of enabling Renault to make more informed production decisions and to reduce stock by an estimated 20 per cent.

Source: Carol Cashmore and Richard Lyall, 1991,
*Business Information Systems and Strategies,*Prentice Hall

Some of the benefits of computer networks to decision makers in business organisations are:

- immediacy

- sharing

- removal of barriers

- better structures

- new business possibilities.

Immediacy

Information processed by one user can be immediately communicated to other users on the network system. Individuals are able to make decisions quickly and effectively because they have immediate access to high quality information.

Sharing

Information can be shared via a central database.

Removal of barriers

Messages can be sent instantly anywhere in the world at any time of the day. A team of people in different parts of the world could reach a consensus on an important decision after discussing it via the network.

Better structures

An organisation can achieve decentralisation while still maintaining strong central control. For example, a clothing company which had factories in 15 different countries managed to reduce its debts by £10,000,000 by making each unit responsible for debt collection. The financial director at head office no longer had to maintain control by holding funds centrally; she could keep a close check on bank balances via the computer network.

New business possibilities

Some organisations owe their very existence to communication networks. The package delivery company Federal Express and American Express are examples here. Other businesses are able to enter new markets because they have created a good network.

Two key disadvantages of networks are incompatibility and threats to security.

Incompatibility

In the past, many information processing systems were created piecemeal as funds became available, as technology developed or as individuals became more aware of the possibilities. This has meant that there have often been problems of incompatibility of both hardware and software.

Threat to security

The widespread use of electronic technology has raised many fears about the security of information. Computer networks mean that many people can gain access to information about, for example, customer details. The information might be deleted accidentally or deliberately – or it might be of a confidential nature and used fraudulently. The organisation has to introduce controls to ensure that certain information can be used by authorised people only. This topic is covered in more detail in section 3 session 1, 'Identifying contingencies'.

summary

▶ Decision makers need information that is appropriate for the choices that they need to make. To make planning decisions, organisations need relevant information about environmental trends; to make control decisions, they need to know how current performance compares with target figures.

▶ To be useful, information should be relevant, supplied in appropriate detail, accurate, complete, timely and effectively presented.

▶ Organisations need to collect, store and communicate three basic types of information: external information, corporate information and internal information.

▶ To meet the needs of decision makers, information flows into an organisation from a vast number of sources. These can be categorised into three main types: human sources, written or manual sources, and information technology sources.

▶ In network organisations, strategic plans are made and resources allocated at the corporate centre. The role of head office is no longer to supervise and monitor the units but to hold them together, to support them and to co-ordinate their efforts.

▶ Network business structures have only been made possible by recent developments in telecommunication and computer technology. They must be supported by a matrix of information channels that link the different units to each other and to head office. Effective decision making demands that information must be available to anyone who needs it as soon as data is collected.

Creative approaches

Objectives

After participating in this session, you should be able to:

▶ explain the meaning and value of creativity for decision making in a business context

▶ identify the characteristics of a creative organisation

▶ differentiate between management beliefs and behaviour that will encourage creativity and those that will not

▶ use a range of techniques for creative decision making.

In working through this session, you will practise the following BTEC common skills:

Managing and developing self	✔
Working with and relating to others	✔
Communicating	✔
Managing tasks and solving problems	✔
Applying numeracy	
Applying technology	
Applying design and creativity	✔

The need for creativity

New ways of thinking about things can release new energies and make all manner of things possible.

Charles Handy, 1989, *The Age of Unreason*, Hutchinson

Thinking creatively is a key technique for generating different options or solutions – the second step of the decision-making process looked at in session 1 of this section. Thinking creatively is the ability to see problems or situations in other ways, to look at them from a different perspective, from another angle – sideways, back to front, even upside down. Creative thinking is in many ways the opposite of the logical, linear way in which managers have often been expected to approach problems or decisions in the past.

In his book *Serious Creativity* (Harper Collins, 1992) Edward de Bono notes two main areas in business where there is a practical need for creativity. First, where there is a problem or a crisis and the organisation or individual cannot proceed without a new idea. For example, a package delivery company is in financial difficulties and is incurring huge bills for maintaining its motorcycle fleet: considerable cost savings are made when it has the idea of selling the bikes to the riders and paying them a use fee.

Second, where there is no pressing problem but a new idea would offer opportunity, advantage and benefit. The chief executive of a life insurance company comes up with the idea of paying out life insurance benefits before the death of the policy holder. This leads to the concept of 'living benefits' – any policy holder who falls sick with a serious illness is immediately entitled to 75 per cent of the benefits that would have been payable on death.

Despite its value, however, there are many misconceptions about creativity.

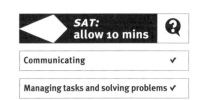

Communicating ✓

Managing tasks and solving problems ✓

ACTIVITY 1

Read the following statements about creativity and creative people.

(a) Creativity is a talent that some people have and others do not.

(b) New ideas just happen by accident, so it is impossible to plan them.

(c) Creative thinking has to be crazy to be effective.

(d) Systematic and deliberate tools can lead to creativity.

(e) It is the job of senior managers to be creative – everyone else should just carry out orders.

Which statements do you believe to be true? Which are false? If you think that the statement is false, explain your reasons.

Commentary...

Statement (a) is false: although some people are naturally more creative than others, everyone has the potential to be creative. Statement (b) is false: it is possible to set out deliberately to generate new ideas. Statement (c) is false: in fact creative thinking is best approached in a rational way and should lead to the generation of ideas that are practical and feasible.

Statement (d) is true: systematic techniques give people the freedom to develop new concepts and perceptions. Statement (e) is false: both managers and subordinates are capable of being creative if they are given the opportunity. In productive organisations, it is the role of senior managers to take the lead in encouraging others to generate ideas and solve problems.

INNOVATION NEEDED

The need for creativity and innovation has been recognised within business organisations for many decades. In *The Practice of Management* (Butterworth Heinemann, 1994), Peter Drucker lists the main areas where innovation is required at the strategic level:

- New products or services are needed to attain **marketing objectives**.

- New products or services will be needed because of technological changes that may make present products **obsolete**.

- **Product improvements** are needed both to attain market objectives and to anticipate expected technological changes.

- New processes and improvements in old processes are needed to satisfy market goals, e.g. manufacturing improvements to make possible the attainment of pricing objectives.

- Innovations and improvements in all major areas of activity – in accounting or design, office management or labour relations – are needed to keep up with the advances in knowledge and skill.

But creativity has never been more vital than in the turbulent, highly competitive business environment of the 1990s. In *Managing in the Next Millennium* (Butterworth Heinemann, 1995), Mike Johnson quotes from an interview with Michael Porter who is (at the time of writing) Professor of Business Administration at Harvard Business School. In the interview, Porter has been arguing that innovation is more important than efficiency and that the Japanese are winning in consumer electronics because they anticipate rather than follow market trends. Porter concludes:

> **If you sit still at any one place you are dead. Because some other country or company with cheaper wages or some other location with hungrier people will come and take the business away from you ... The only way to be competitive is to progress.**

The creative organisation

Improving the creative aspects of decision making depends on an organisation's capacity to bring about the kind of culture where creativity is encouraged and valued.

Like individuals, few organisations are naturally creative, even if they are lucky enough to have one or two highly creative people in positions of power. The really successful organisations are those that set out deliberately to develop and make the best possible use of people's capacity to think of new ideas. In an article in *Management Today* (July 1995), John Thackray describes the experience of Eclipse, a 50-year-old 550-person capital goods manufacturing company, specialising in industrial heat treatment. This organisation has gone out of its way to make creativity systemic.

> **Every employee is expected to be entirely self-motivating. The company demands that all workers have and stick to a personal two-year self-development plan for additional education and enrichment experiences – a quarter of these to be in areas unrelated to work tasks.**
>
> **'Creativity and innovation is a function of connecting ideas, people and systems that the world has never seen connected before,' says John Myers, Eclipse's vice president of human resources. As part of his obligation, Myers took up computer studies and has also delved into the technology and markets for catalytic converters – just in case this knowledge is useful to the company in future.**

Source: John Thackray, 1995, 'That Vital Spark', in *Management Today*, July

Creative organisations are able to recognise and exploit the diverse talents of their members, rather than insisting on set processes and procedures. Furthermore, organisations that want to encourage creativity build distinct types of systems and structures which allow creative behaviour to take place and reward it when it happens.

ACTIVITY 2

Put a circle around the nine words or phrases in the following list that you think best describe the climate that exists within a creative organisation.

open	penalises failure	diversified
complacent	ready to experiment	prescriptive
decentralised	original	indifferent
cautious	directive	rewards ideas
dislikes risks	allows eccentricity	flexible
a tight ship	dislikes long-term plans	
repressive	encourages outside contacts	

Commentary...

The words and phrases that you should have picked out are: open, diversified, ready to experiment, decentralised, original, rewards ideas, allows eccentricity, flexible and encourages outside contacts.

During the 1980s, creativity development used to be targeted at R&D, marketing, advertising and public relations; it was thought that these functions would find it easier and more useful to develop creativity than any others in the organisation. In the 1990s, however, an increasing number of businesses have been trying to develop creativity among clerical staff, engineers and computer information systems personnel. John Thackray notes:

> There is now an awareness that creativity isn't necessarily Big Bang and that the corporation can benefit from a lot of small bangs, even squeaks.

Source: John Thackray, 1995, 'That Vital Spark', in *Management Today*, July

Encouraging creativity

It is not enough for the organisation to evolve structures and systems that develop creativity; managers also have to provide the sort of environment that will encourage creative decision making within their areas of responsibility. One factor that makes an important contribution is the tone of personal relationships that managers generate within their teams.

Managers can help people to become creative decision makers by:

- showing respect for them

- showing empathy

- being genuine.

Showing **respect** means letting other people know they are valued for what they are and accepted for their uniqueness and individuality. **Empathy** is the ability to see things from others' points of view and to communicate that understanding. **Genuineness** is self-knowledge, being oneself and the ability to be honest and sincere.

The activity which follows asks you to think about your own past experiences of working relationships and about the effects these have had on your performance.

ACTIVITY 3

Think about your experience in school, college, in a part-time job or in a sporting or leisure activity – any situation where your ability to perform well mattered. Think about your own experience for a few minutes and identify an occasion when good working relationships contributed to a task you were trying to achieve.

Now pick out an example of how poor working relationships hindered your efforts.

EXERCISE:
allow 10 mins

| Managing and developing self | ✔ |
| Working with and relating to others | ✔ |

Commentary...

You may have discovered, like many others, that the quality of your working relationships directly affected your motivation and your ability to commit yourself to a particular task.

Good relationships allow people to perform well by:

- encouraging regular and open communication

- making them confident that their ideas and suggestions will be listened to and considered

- allowing people to admit any lack of expertise, knowing that support will be provided for any training needs

- encouraging participation

- involving them in the decision-making process.

Poor relationships, on the other hand, hinder effective performance because of:

- distrust and an unwillingness to communicate

- hostility between individuals

- situations in which decisions cannot be reached because conflicts cannot be resolved.

BREAKING DOWN THE BARRIERS

Barriers between management and staff cause bad relationships in the workplace and make people reluctant to come up with new ideas. However, once trust, openness and mutual respect are allowed to develop, these barriers do come down.

If subordinates trust their managers and leaders, they will feel safe enough to take a step into the unknown. They will be able to afford the risk of making mistakes as they voice their creative ideas and put them into practice. But if they have miscalculated – if their trust is betrayed and their mistakes are punished – they will put up defences which may prove difficult to overcome a second time.

Managers' values and beliefs about people affect the extent to which they feel able to promote creativity and freedom to take risks. The following exercise was devised as a way of helping managers to identify their own beliefs about people. Try it for yourself.

ACTIVITY 4

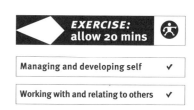

EXERCISE:
allow 20 mins

Managing and developing self ✔

Working with and relating to others ✔

Do this exercise independently and then discuss your findings with others in a small group.

The following statements are pairs of opposing opinions about work and attitudes. Consider each pair and then mark the number on the scale which represents your point of view on the spectrum between the two extremes.

People are paid not to think.	1	2	3	4	People are intelligent, curious and responsible.
People are lacking in creative ideas.	1	2	3	4	Many people are capable of creating good ideas.
People work solely for money.	1	2	3	4	People look for job satisfaction as well as money.
People are all the same.	1	2	3	4	People are individuals.
Managers manage; team members work.	1	2	3	4	Managers and team members are both trying to achieve good results.
People shun responsibility for their work.	1	2	3	4	People like to take responsibility for what they do.
Discipline and control get the best results.	1	2	3	4	People respond best when given freedom of action.
Punishments get results.	1	2	3	4	Excessive punishments are counter productive.
Add up your scores and note the total here:					

Commentary...

This activity is based on the research carried out by Douglas McGregor which he reported in his book *The Human Side of Enterprise* (Penguin Books, 1987). He identified two distinct and opposite management styles and called the set of assumptions on which each is based 'Theory X' and 'Theory Y'.

Place your total score on the scale below to find out which style you tend towards.

Theory X					**Theory Y**	
8	12	16	20	24	28	32

Theory X managers believe that people:

- have an inborn dislike for work

- must be controlled, directed and threatened before they will make any sort of effort

- prefer to be told what to do and avoid taking responsibility.

These managers are likely to rule by fear, giving orders and threatening punishment.

Theory Y managers believe that people:

- enjoy physical and mental effort just as much as leisure activities or resting

- will motivate themselves if they are committed to achieving something

- will, under the right conditions, seek and accept responsibility

- are naturally imaginative, creative and ingenious.

These managers are likely to take a positive view of others and will encourage responsibility and trust.

McGregor found that Theory Y managers tended to produce better results than Theory X leaders. Their teams were more creative and innovative, and had fewer staff problems. Few managers, however, are entirely Theory X or Theory Y.

Techniques for creative decision making

We continue this session with a brief look at some of the main techniques used within organisations for creative decision making or problem solving. Some of these approaches are more useful if they are undertaken by a group; others can be carried out by individuals working alone.

Most people are creative in some way, and many will have had original and valuable thoughts about the work which occupies a large proportion of their lives. However, many are also easily inhibited when placed in a group, and require a supportive and non-critical environment in order to be able to express themselves. A quiet room with space to move about, comfortable chairs arranged in a semicircle, flip charts and coloured pens do much to encourage innovative thought processes. Most organisations have suitable training rooms or conference rooms; some even have specially designed facilities with visual aids and projection equipment.

> **The most important thing with regard to creativity is to have methodical processes to enhance individual and group creativity. Creativity isn't just something that happens to a group of bright people.**
>
> Product development manager

BRAINSTORMING

Brainstorming is an activity that harnesses the dynamic energy of a group to create ideas, make decisions or solve problems. Members of the group are asked to suggest ideas relating to the problem or situation, and to be as free as possible in their thinking. One of the group (often the team leader or manager) writes down the suggestions as they are produced, preferably using a flipchart. This is so that everyone can see what has gone before and allow associations and links to flow freely.

The 'rules' of brainstorming are as follows:

- Write down exactly what people say.

- Do not stop to discuss or evaluate suggestions during the brainstorm, as this interrupts the free flow of ideas.

- The time to categorise and evaluate all the suggestions is when the brainstorm is complete. At this point the group draws up a shortlist of the most feasible ideas.

This next activity will enable you to practise brainstorming, following the above rules carefully.

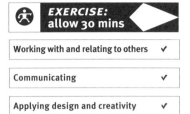

EXERCISE:
allow 30 mins

Working with and relating to others	✓
Communicating	✓
Applying design and creativity	✓

ACTIVITY 5

Provide a few paper-clips for each person in a group of between three and six people. Ask them to look at their paper-clips, touch and manipulate them. Then ask the group to think of all the things that they could do with paper-clips.

Build up a list on the flip chart – make this fun, fast and lively. Write down all the ideas, even the oddest ones; if no crazy ideas emerge introduce some of your own.

When ideas seem to have dried up, ask for just one more item from each person to make sure that nothing has been held back.

Commentary...

When you have completed the activity discuss the outcome with the group. How many ideas emerged in the 10 minutes or so that it took to complete the brainstorm?

What about the range of ideas? Groups have been known to cover everything from fashion to gardening and from film making to weaponry.

Consider the wild ideas. Although these might not be practicable, they might stimulate other suggestions or alert the group to aspects they would not otherwise think of. For example, although it might be 'weird' to think of 'making jewellery' with paper-clips, it is perfectly feasible to use them for dolls or as part of a fancy dress costume. Again, although you may not like to use a paper-clip 'as a weapon', this might remind you of the fact that paper-clips can be dangerous.

The next step in a brainstorming session would be to sift through the suggestions, perhaps discarding the ones which are not feasible. The group would next choose three or four ideas that it liked best and then, through a process of discussion and refining, finally decide which one to adopt and put into practice.

IDEAS WRITING

This is similar to brainstorming except that people write their ideas down instead of contributing to a communal list. Some people prefer to work individually like this because they are not distracted by other people's thought processes. Others miss the stimulus that can come from working in a group.

Members can either write lists on ordinary paper or they can note individual items on post-it notes. The advantage of the list system is that an extra list can be provided by the group leader and left in the middle of the group. When members run out of ideas, they can exchange their own list with the one from the centre. This usually stimulates a few more thoughts. The advantage of the post-its is that these can be displayed for all to see on a white board and easily arranged into clusters.

ACTIVITY 6

Once again, do this activity in a group of between three and six people, this time using one of the 'ideas writing' techniques described above.

Imagine you are the manager in a company where the accident record has reached an all time high. Gather a group together to 'ideas write' some ideas for making people more safety conscious. You will need to start by identifying the kind of company you work in and what kinds of accidents have been occurring.

After brainstorming, evaluating and discussing the ideas that come up, identify the one that you think is the best. Write this idea in the space below, saying why the group thinks this the best idea, what the benefits would be and for whom.

Also reflect on the creative process. What are the benefits of brainstorming and ideas writing as creative techniques? Did you notice any problems related to this approach? If so, what are they?

EXERCISE:
allow 1 hour

Working with and relating to others	✔
Communicating	✔
Applying design and creativity	✔

Commentary...

Brainstorming and similar techniques were originally designed for use in the advertising industry. Their purpose was to allow groups of people to 'bounce ideas off each other' – to have someone else's remark stimulate your own thinking. In this way, the group should come up with a greater number of innovative ideas than would have been possible if individuals were working alone. When groups use creative techniques, it is valuable because they feel ownership of the ideas they come up with. People often enjoy working in groups – if the techniques are well executed they can be fast, exhilarating and fun.

Some people think that groups are a slow, inefficient way of reaching the desired outcome. In a group, someone talks and others listen or a member of a group may feel obliged to elaborate on an idea if he or she feels that it has not been fully understood by the others. Then there is the tendency to make frivolous remarks to ease the tension, to shock or to get a laugh.

Some of the other techniques that we describe in this session counteract the problems that some people have with group brainstorming.

MIND MAPS

Mind Mapping is a technique devised by Tony Buzan which challenges traditional ways of thinking and listing information. It builds on scientific research into the workings of the human brain which has revealed the importance of using colour, images and key words to aid the free association of ideas. Mind Mapping has many uses and applications, but here we are concerned with using it as a tool for thinking creatively and solving problems.

> Because of the large amount of association involved in Mind
> Maps, they can be very creative; they tend to generate new ideas
> and associations that have not been thought of before. Every
> item in a map is in effect the centre of another map, and one
> could go on generating maps ad infinitum.

Peter Russel, 1979, The Brain Book, Routledge & Kegan Paul

Making Mind Maps involves both sides of the brain – the logical left side and the imaginative right side. Research by neurologists has shown that certain aspects of our thinking and emotions are associated with one or other of the two halves of the brain: the left side dealing with logic, words, reasoning, numbers, analysis etc., while the right side is linked to areas such as rhythm, images, imagination, colour, daydreaming or patterns.

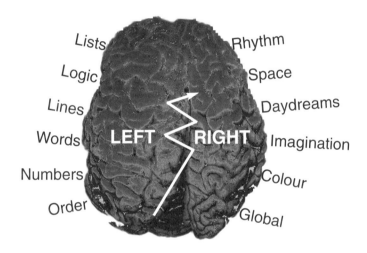

FIGURE 3.1: *The left and right halves of the brain.*

Most of us have been trained by an educational system that focuses on reasoning and the logical progression of ideas to rely heavily on the left side of our brains. We often find it difficult to use the right side effectively. However, when it is stimulated and encouraged to work in conjunction with the left side, the overall result is an increase in creativity and problem-solving skills.

Mind Mapping generates information in a form that mirrors the way the brain actually functions, rather than in the vertical, logical lists we are more normally accustomed to. Ideas are therefore shown as coloured images and key words branching out from a central theme.

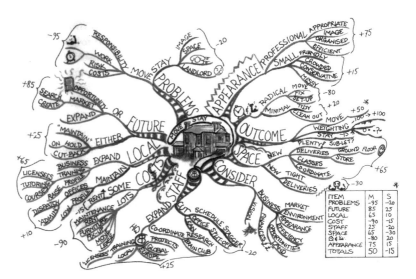

FIGURE 3.2: *A Mind Map drawn by Vanda North, director of Buzan Centres Ltd, helping her to decide whether or not to move her business.*

This is how the Mind Map in figure 3.2 was constructed. The creator started with a coloured image of the core subject in the centre – a picture representing the topic about which she had to make a decision. In this case, she was thinking about whether to move premises or to stay where she was.

She then let her mind flow freely around this image. First she printed the main themes (appearance, outcomes, space and so on) on a thick curved line connected to the central topic. Then she added a second level of thought with words or images connected to the main branch that triggered them. Under problems, for example, she has written 'move' and 'stay' and under appearance she has 'professional' and 'small'; these lines are thinner than the main branches and words are again printed.

The Mind Mapper has continued to add third and fourth levels as the thoughts came to her, using images as much as she could. Then she weighted each key word by giving them a number from 1 to 100. Finally she added the scores up to find out which one had the highest total.

ACTIVITY 7

Imagine that you run a small picture-framing business from a workshop at the rear of your house. Until recently, orders have come in steadily and you have coped very well with the help of your spouse who looks after the bookkeeping. However, you are starting to receive more work than you can handle easily and space is becoming very cramped because you are buying in extra stock to meet the demand.

You have to decide whether to move to a larger premises and perhaps take on extra staff. Draw a mind map that draws out some of the issues involved in expanding the business in this way. You will find it valuable to draw this map on a separate sheet of paper, but you might make a start using the box below.

Commentary...

Your mind map may include some of the following points:

- Costs – rent, rates, power, new stationery (letters, business cards, etc.), telephone

- Risks – loan, mortgage, stable demand?, lifestyle

- Benefits – more work and/or money, larger space, business development, interest

- Image – professional, appropriate, promotional

- Staff – administration, production, marketing

Remember, there are no right or wrong mind maps. The one that you have produced will probably be very different from those of others' thinking about the same subject; this merely reflects your different perspectives and ideas. Mind maps are also never complete. You can make your brain continue to explore the topic by adding extra branches.

LATERAL THINKING

The simplest way to describe lateral thinking is to say: 'You cannot dig a hole in a different place by digging the same hole deeper.' This emphasises the searching for different approaches and different ways of looking at things.

Edward de Bono, 1992, *Serious Creativity*, Harper Collins

Lateral thinking is a term that was invented by Edward de Bono in 1967. De Bono suggests that, whereas conventional 'vertical thinking' requires you to take up an initial position and then build (or dig down) logically on that basis, 'lateral thinking' allows you to move sideways, to try different perceptions and different entry points. Logic is concerned with 'the truth', with what is, but lateral thinking is more concerned with possibilities, with what might be. Lateral thinking is also about exploring and changing perceptions and concepts.

There are many techniques for lateral thinking, and we only have space to look at some of the more widely used ones here:

- checking assumptions

- six thinking hats

- provocations.

CHECKING ASSUMPTIONS

One of the overall blocks to creativity is being stuck with assumptions that are not necessarily valid. Edward de Bono has provided us with a technique for 'moving outside the square' by looking at the constraints that define a problem. He sees the constraints around a situation as being defined by five factors:

1. the dominant idea

2. the tethering factors

3. the polarising factors

4. the boundaries

5. the assumptions.

For example, suppose we have a company manufacturing widgets in a rural area. The **dominant idea** directs the approach to a problem and may be stated explicitly or merely implied. It may well be couched in language such as 'we are a manufacturing company', 'we are responsible for the well-being of the neighbourhood, and are responsible citizens'.

The dominant idea may be powerful, but the **tethering factor** may be a small almost insignificant idea. An example could be that the chief executive officer is on the Board of Governors of a local school and is expected to award the prizes every year. Any change in policy towards local employment could well embarrass the relationship. We may well wish to consider the priorities of running a business against this tethering factor.

Polarising factors are constraints disguised as 'either/or'. An organisation could be either a manufacturer or an importer of finished goods. Polarising factors dismiss the possibility of the halfway house – for instance, a part-finished goods assembler.

Boundaries form the framework within which the problem is supposed to be considered. In our example, we may think of these in terms of the position of the shareholders or the bank – 'we have to live within the constraints set by the bank', 'the shareholders have bought into a UK based company'. The statement may be true but should be checked.

If boundaries are the limits of the ideas, **assumptions** are the building blocks that created the boundaries. We assume that the bank is not open to negotiation and that the shareholders will not be open to reasoned argument.

Using a non-judgmental questioning of the five factors we can redesign the problem creatively and have a chance of reaching new solutions.

TECHNIQUES FOR CREATIVE
DECISION MAKING

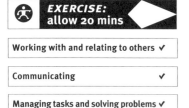

EXERCISE:
allow 20 mins

| Working with and relating to others ✔ |
| Communicating ✔ |
| Managing tasks and solving problems ✔ |

ACTIVITY 8

With others in a small group, think of an activity you, your friends or your college has been involved in for some time. You may select the issue of going to the same place for a holiday or the fact that your college organises an event in a certain way 'because we have always done it like that'.

Work through the de Bono assumption analysis and question each assumption. Identify the dominant idea, any tethering factors, polarising factors, the boundaries and assumptions.

Commentary...

Edward de Bono notes that it is impossible to examine all the constraints. Nevertheless, if you set them out logically like this you will become more aware of the cage within which you are operating. You will see more easily whether this particular cage is relevant for the present time and place.

The Ford Motor Company, in a vigorous campaign to increase engineering creativity in its EQUIP programme, demands that the minutes of important meetings are circulated well in advance and that each meeting starts by a sharing of the assumptions each participant brings to the items on the agenda. The process works well – saving time and allowing for new approaches.

SIX THINKING HATS

This simple but powerful framework is used by many organisations to make meetings more productive and to encourage people to think more broadly and creatively when they are faced with challenging decisions.

The technique is based on the view that there are six different types of thinking, each one associated with a different colour.

1. **White hat thinking** is to do with data and information. When someone asks for white hat thinking at a meeting, he or she is asking everyone to focus completely on the information available to make a decision or how this information might be obtained.

2. **Red hat thinking** is concerned with feelings, intuition and emotions. The red hat gives people permission to reveal their feelings without any need to justify them. Intuition may sometimes be valuable even if the reasons for it cannot be expressed at first.

3. **Black hat thinking** is about caution and critical judgement. The black hat is valuable because it helps decision makers to avoid making silly mistakes. Although the black hat is useful, it should not be overused because it can kill creativity.

4. **Yellow hat thinking** is for optimism and taking a positive point of view. The yellow hat looks for benefits and for ways of making ideas work. This hat is not so easy to use as the black hat; it sometimes takes time and effort to see the positive side of things.

5. **Green hat thinking** makes it possible to ask directly for creative effort. The green hat makes time available to think of new ideas, for additional alternatives, for possibilities and hypotheses.

6. **Blue hat thinking** is to do with organising and controlling the thinking process so that it becomes more productive. This hat is usually put on by the chairperson or facilitator of the meeting but other participants can step in and make a blue hat observation about the way the meeting is going.

TECHNIQUES FOR CREATIVE
DECISION MAKING

USING THE HATS TO EXPLORE IDEAS

The Western tradition insists that we try to move forward in a discussion by means of position taking and argument. 'A' has a point of view and 'B' disagrees. Too often the protagonists become locked into their positions and become more interested in winning the argument than in exploring the subject.

With the six thinking hats method both 'A' and 'B' can wear the black hat at the same time to find out the dangers. Both 'A' and 'B' can wear the yellow hat to explore the benefits and so on. Instead of adversarial thinking there is co-operative exploration.

Source: Edward de Bono, 1992, *Serious Creativity*, Harper Collins, p.81

Although it is true that some people are naturally more skilled at one type of thinking than the others, the coloured hats are not intended to describe the people involved. They refer rather to the type of thinking behaviour that may be appropriate in generating ideas, moving the discussion on or making a decision. The purpose of the six hats is that everyone should make an effort to wear all six hats as and when they are required to do so by the group. In this way individuals will not become locked into, say, a black hat or a green hat thinking style.

The power of the hats is that they allow decision makers to get away from arguments and to move towards more productive discussions. Someone who does not like an idea may be challenged to wear a yellow hat and think of points in favour of it. Likewise someone who is enthusiastic about an idea may have to look at the difficulties connected with it. Quite often people have changed their point of view when using the thinking hats approach.

? **SAT:**
allow 10 mins

Managing tasks and solving problems ✔

ACTIVITY 9

Specify which hats the following speakers are wearing.

Speaker	Hat
1 We tried that before and it did not work.	
2 We don't have enough information. How shall we find more?	
3 We have spent the last 10 minutes looking for someone to blame.	
4 Perhaps some new ideas would help. Shall we think of some alternatives?	
5 It's true that energy is expensive but this would force us to be more efficient.	
6 Let's get all the facts straight before we go any further.	
7 I think we should review where we've got to before we go any further.	
8 I'm not sure why, but it's my feeling that this idea will work.	

Commentary...

Now check your answers: the first statement shows black hat thinking; the second, white hat thinking; the third, blue; the fourth, green; the fifth, yellow; the sixth, white; the seventh, blue; and, the eighth, red hat thinking.

The Six Thinking Hats method is a useful approach for making thinking more productive and discussions less adversarial within a business organisation. The green hat may be used as a specific request for creative effort when decisions are being made, but it does not state how that creativity should be arrived at. The group may decide to use any one of a number of creative techniques at this point, including those discussed in this section.

PROVOCATIONS

This technique involves putting forward provocative statements to stimulate creativity in the mind. De Bono invented the word 'po' to signal the fact that a deliberately provocative statement is being made. For example, if someone were to suggest that cars have square wheels, much time would be wasted in criticising and deriding such a mad idea. But if you say 'Po, cars have square wheels' it is obvious that the statement is intended as a provocation.

> Words like hy(po)thesis, sup(po)se, (po)ssible and (po)etry all indicate the 'forward use' of a statement. We make the statement and then see where it takes us. This is the opposite of prose and description in which we seek to show something as it is now. The syllable 'po' is therefore extracted from such words and formalised as a symbol for provocation.

> Edward de Bono, 1992, *Serious Creativity,* Harper Collins, p.145

There is a story that someone wrote to Robert Watson Watt (the inventor of radar) in the late 1930s and suggested that the Ministry of Defence made a radio wave strong enough to shoot down aircraft. Watt rejected the crazy idea on the spot but his assistant used it as a provocation and suggested that perhaps the reflection of the radio wave might be able to detect aircraft. This is how the concept of radar came into being – a piece of technology that was to prove invaluable during the Second World War.

There are three main approaches to provocation:

- escape provocation
- reversal
- exaggeration.

Escape provocation entails spelling out the things that we take for granted in any situation and then denying, negating or escaping from these aspects:

- We take for granted that restaurants have menus.
- Po, restaurants do not have menus.

From this provocation you could proceed in a variety of directions. You could create the idea of a restaurant which gives diners a list of available ingredients and allows them to order what they want within those limits. Or you could think of a restaurant where the chef prepares just one starter, one main course and one sweet course, giving diners little or no choice. In fact, some restaurants do run along these lines.

Reversal involves reversing the usual direction in which things are done:

- I have orange juice for breakfast.
- Po, the orange juice has me for breakfast.

This crazy idea might lead you to visualise falling into a huge bath of juice and coming up smelling of oranges! You might go on to imagine having a special attachment on the shower head that would take sticks of perfume.

USING 'PO' FOR PRODUCT DEVELOPMENT

At least one of Union Carbide Chemical's fledgling businesses came out of reversing conventional approaches – super critical carbon dioxide for paints and solvents. In response to regulations limiting the use of some solvents in coating, the idea was first put forward to use a gas, like carbon dioxide. When the idea was first aired, people just laughed and hooted. It seemed off the wall. It was argued that there are all sorts of reasons why you can't use a gas in paint. Eventually, with special chemical agents and equipment to apply the gas, it turned out to be feasible.

Source: John Thackray, 1995, 'That Vital Spark' in *Management Today*, July, p.57

Edward de Bono gives the following example of a 'po' derived from **exaggeration** that worked in practice:

> The Swedish Film Institute once came to see me to ask how they might raise money for films. Po, each cinema ticket costs $100. (This is, of course, an exaggeration.) This leads to the idea that for first-run films there is a single mechanism whereby viewers can go back to the box office and invest money directly in the film they have just seen. They would now have the chance to assess the product – as distinct from investing in advance. They would also become ambassadors for the film and would encourage others to see the film. This investment would pay back the initial risk takers so reducing their risk and encouraging initial investment.
>
> Edward be Bono, 1992, Serious Creativity, Harper Collins

Once the technique of provocation is established and understood, it can become part of the creative decision-making process. Many organisations find that it useful to encourage people to come up with provocative ideas if only because this 'jerks their minds out of the usual grooves'.

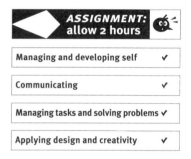

ASSIGNMENT: allow 2 hours	
Managing and developing self	✔
Communicating	✔
Managing tasks and solving problems	✔
Applying design and creativity	✔

ACTIVITY 10

Imagine that you are one of a team of three supervisors in a light engineering factory in the West Midlands. You have noticed that your team's productivity has started to fall recently and morale seems to be very low too. Recently two of your best workers, both black, have complained to you that some of their team mates have started taunting and jeering at them, making their lives miserable in a number of ways.

Use one or more of the techniques described in this section to decide what to do in this situation. Then write a report of approximately 1,500 words covering the following areas:

- What is the problem or what might the problem be?

- What are your objectives in solving this problem?

- What options are open to you to solve the problem?

Include in your report a description of the method or methods you used to generate these options.

Write your report on separate paper. Use the box below to note your main ideas.

TECHNIQUES FOR CREATIVE
DECISION MAKING

summary

▶ Thinking creatively is the ability to see problems or situations in other ways, to look at them from a different perspective, from another angle – sideways, back to front, even upside down.

▶ The really successful organisations are those that set out deliberately to develop and make the best possible use of people's capacity to think of new ideas.

▶ It is not enough for the organisation to evolve structures and systems that develop creativity; managers have to provide the sort of environment that will encourage creative decision making within their areas of responsibility.

▶ Brainstorming is an activity that harnesses the dynamic energy of a group to create ideas, make decisions or solve problems. Members of the group are asked to suggest ideas relating to the problem or situation, and to be as free as possible in their thinking.

▶ Mind mapping is a technique devised by Tony Buzan which challenges traditional ways of thinking and listing information. It builds on scientific research into the workings of human brain.

▶ Logic is concerned with 'the truth', with what is; lateral thinking is more concerned with possibilities, with what might be. Lateral thinking is also about exploring and changing perceptions and concepts.

▶ There are many techniques for lateral thinking including checking assumptions, six thinking hats and provocations.

Choosing between options

Objectives

After participating in this session, you should be able to:

▶ describe the criteria that can be used to evaluate different options

▶ analyse the acceptability of an option

▶ identify the factors that influence decision makers' personal perceptions

▶ explain how values influence decisions

▶ compare different methods of making choices.

In working through this session, you will practise the following BTEC common skills:

Managing and developing self	✔
Working with and relating to others	
Communicating	✔
Managing tasks and solving problems	✔
Applying numeracy	
Applying technology	
Applying design and creativity	

Evaluating options

Having generated a number of options, the next step in the decision-making process is to evaluate the most suitable ones. For routine or urgent decisions, this evaluation may be made very quickly and informally by an individual manager. For more problematic decisions or decisions that will have a significant impact on the business, however, the process of evaluation has to be approached in a more systematic way.

The exact nature of the factors to be evaluated will depend on the decision being made. However, three groups of evaluation criteria are commonly used:

- feasibility

- acceptability

- risk.

FEASIBILITY

Businesses evaluate the **feasibility** of an option by considering:

- the skills required to implement it

- its effects on the capacity of the operation

- the financial requirements required to implement it.

Organisations have to decide whether they have the required expertise to cope with the implications of a particular decision. If an option involves a big move, such as restructuring, going into a new market or taking a new approach, there may well be a **skills gap**. For example, a children's book company that had always sold direct to the trade is considering whether to set up a sales team in the field that would co-ordinate book parties and exhibitions in schools. One of the first factors the organisation has to face is whether it has sufficient skills within the company to cope with this type of work. After some thought and analysis, the company decides to classify the skills needed as marketing, selling, advertising, customer contact, team leadership and project management. Table 4.1 shows the results of the company's investigation of existing skills. Having identified any skills gaps, the company can more easily decide whether the option under consideration is feasible.

Skill	Plenty of experience	Some experience	No experience
Marketing	√		
Selling	√		
Advertising		√	
Customer contact		√	
Team leadership			√
Project management			√

TABLE 4.1: *Skills audit*

Organisations have to consider their capacity to implement each option. They need to determine the quantities of human and material resources required for each option under consideration. The numbers of people and facilities required can be arrived at by identifying any gaps between the resources needed to meet existing demand and the resources needed to meet demand if the option is selected.

In the case of the book company, the task is to estimate the amount of work involved in the option under consideration. It could do this by asking staff to work out how many person/weeks would be required to fulfil each part of the proposed new project. The company can then compare this with its current work commitment to arrive at a picture of the additional capacity required.

Cost is frequently the most important feasibility criterion. Organisations need to know whether they can afford a particular option before they accept or reject it. Important strategic decisions will, of course, have an effect on the financial planning for whole organisation, whereas operational or routine decisions may only have an impact on one department's budget or part of a budget.

Decision makers need to take several different costs into account:

- monetary costs

- non-monetary costs

- opportunity costs.

Monetary costs are relatively easy to analyse if they are one-off costs. However, for a project such as the one the book company is contemplating the costs will be incurred over the entire financial year. A more accurate picture is obtained if the total outflow of cash as it will occur is compared with the estimated inflow of cash. In this way, the company will be able to calculate how much money it needs to borrow to implement the option and when.

A further monetary cost is interest on finances borrowed. This can only be included in the total costing when it is decided how much cash is required, when it is required and how it is to be raised.

A number of factors could be considered as **non-monetary costs.** Important ones could be the cost of using valuable working or storage space, the costs associated with increased travelling or stress and the costs to the families of the people involved in big projects.

Opportunity costs are the costs of pursuing one option rather than another. For example, by implementing the option of selling books in the field the book company may be giving up the alternative opportunity of organising a mail-order service. Another cost might be the lost opportunity to make the most of what the company is involved in at the moment. It might be that the option cannot be implemented without distracting considerably from current activities.

The accurate financial evaluation of an option is a complex task which involves predicting both the monetary and non-monetary costs and benefits that will arise from a decision. To learn more about this aspect of decision making, you could consult the companion workbook in this series: *Managing Finance and Information*.

ACCEPTABILITY

The acceptability of an option is the extent to which it fulfils the original objectives of the decision. In an operational context these objectives are likely to relate to organisation's operational performance objectives.

As a basis for asking questions about the acceptability of various decision options, managers could use some categories of operational objectives identified in *Making Management Decisions* by Cook and Slack (2nd edn, 1991, Prentice Hall):

- **Technical specification** – does the option improve products and services or bring them closer to what customers want?

- **Quality** – does the option reduce errors or help to get things right first time?

- **Responsiveness** – does the option shorten the time customers have to wait for their goods and services?

- **Dependability** – does the option increase the chances of things happening when they are supposed to happen?

● **Flexibility** – does the option increase the flexibility of the operation, in terms of the range of things that can be done or the speed of doing them?

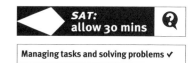

Managing tasks and solving problems ✔

ACTIVITY 1

Use the criteria and questions given above to analyse the acceptability of the option being considered by the children's book company. Write a short report on your evaluation and summarise your ideas in the box below.

Commentary...

You may have included some of the following points in your report:

Technical specification: The option under consideration brings the company's products closer to those customers who never normally consider going into book shops. It will enable buyers to peruse products in a neighbour's house or in their child's school where they will feel more relaxed and able to consider the books at their leisure.

Quality: The option will improve the quality of service provided because it will be both immediate and personal. However, it does nothing to reduce production or administrative errors.

Responsiveness: The option increases responsiveness in some cases because customers will be able to buy directly from the stock held by regional organisers and party planners. In other cases, however, customers will have to order books.

Dependability: Because responsibility will be devolved to the lowest level in this part of the operation, it is expected that the service will be highly dependable. Party organisers, in particular, will trade to a great extent on their personal service and reliability.

Flexibility: The option increases the flexibility of the organisation's marketing department. It is expected that increased profits will accrue because the company's products will be presented to a greater number of potential customers.

RISK

One of the most straightforward ways of analysing risk is to assess the worst possible outcome of the option; this is sometimes called assessing the downside risk of an option. If the organisation is willing to accept the consequences of that risk then it can go ahead with the option. If, on the other hand, it decides that the downside outcomes would be too great to bear, it might reject that option – even though the expected pay-offs in the event of a favourable outcome are high. Decision makers would, of course, have to take into account the degree of likelihood that the risk will actually become reality.

Cook and Slack discuss the **portfolio approach** to risk used by members of the world's stock markets. The total 'portfolio of risk' of an organisation is the degree of risk involved in its recent decisions and the amount of money invested in each decision.

> Suppose two activities are subject in the same way to exactly the same set of uncontrollable factors. If the pay-off from one activity declines, then so will the pay-off from the other – both eggs will be in the same basket. But if the uncontrollable factors in the decision influence the two activities in opposite directions then a reduction in the pay-off from one activity will be

accompanied by an increase in the pay-off from the other ... Choosing options which benefit from the things which threaten existing investments will decrease the portfolio's total risk.

Cook, S. and Slack, N., 1991, *Making Management Decisions*, 2nd edn, Prentice Hall

We discuss risk analysis in session 2 of section 3 of this module.

Choice and the individual

Because of the importance of decision making in a business context, organisations strive continuously to improve both the quality of the information available and the processes by which those decisions are made. It is almost impossible, however, to imagine a situation in which for any given choice, decision makers have perfect knowledge both about the alternative options and the consequences of those options. Therefore they can rarely, if ever, make a totally rational judgement about the relative merits of those options.

PERCEPTIONS

When they have to make decisions people tend to use their personal perception of the situation as a basis for making a judgement. The picture that they build up is created from a whole range of factors.

FIGURE 4.1: *Factors that contribute to perception.*

Perception has a particular importance in decision making. This is the process by which people interpret the data they receive through their senses. Once an individual has processed data, it is translated into thought patterns or behaviour. Problems arise because everyone has their own unique perception of how they see the real world. For example, when asked to decide whether or not to accept a new contract that offers a considerable pay rise in return for a reduction in holiday entitlement:

- one manager views this proposal as unacceptable pressure and exploitation

- a second manager welcomes the opportunity to earn more money and make a greater contribution to the success of the business

- a third manager might be willing to accept the new contract if it also provides for flexibility in the hours worked and holidays taken.

Each of the managers perceives the same situation in a completely different way and as their perceptions become their 'reality' of the situation, they are likely to react accordingly. If you want your own examples of how people perceive things differently, compare your perceptions of events or people with others who experienced or saw them at the same time as you.

In their book *Making Management Decisions*, Cook and Slack argue that we try to organise information in different ways to compensate for the unreliability of our perceptions. These efforts to close the gaps in our perceptions are called **closure mechanisms**:

- **Categorising** – here, we simply relate decisions to other problems or experiences we have had in the past. By looking for similarities, we can organise our perception of the present decision by adding to it assumptions that are based on past experience. A simple example would be where a business decides not to purchase equipment from a particular supplier because the last time it did so the supplier failed to provide adequate after-sales service.

- **Stereotyping** – we often evaluate people on the basis of one characteristic such as gender, race or disability, and then proceed to base our actions on our beliefs about all individuals who have that characteristic. In the early 1980s, an Irish job applicant took a major national organisation to the Industrial Tribunal because the interviewer implied that all Irishmen drink large amounts of Guinness. The applicant was awarded substantial compensation by the court.

- **Perceptual defence** – this simply means screening out the stimuli that do not fit our preferred view of the situation or the decision. If we are particularly enthusiastic about a particular course of action, we may be blinded to some of the negative factors.

- **Set or expectancy** – in many situations, we see what we expect to see. Sometimes our expectations are coloured by our own needs for a particular outcome. At others, the physical or emotional circumstances of the decision will affect what stimuli are seen as being important.

It is interesting to note that all these closure mechanisms may themselves be aspects of our subjective perceptions! Nevertheless, before making decisions, you will find it useful to be aware of the mechanisms that you use to filter information.

ACTIVITY 2

Think of a big decision you have made recently and make some notes about how your judgement may have been influenced by the four factors – categorising, stereotyping, perceptual defence, set or expectancy – described above.

SAT: allow 30 mins

Managing and developing self ✔

Commentary...

The chances are that you were affected by at least two of the perception closure mechanisms described here. This is what one student said about his decision to apply for a place at Oxford and Cambridge Universities.

I discussed my application with my tutor and she said I should go ahead – I know I can do it if I really work hard over the next six months. I was determined to get 'A's at GCSE and showed myself capable of that (categorising). One tutor pointed out that if I do get there I may find myself under a lot of pressure as regards work, achieving academic excellence and so on. But I have a good friend at Oxford and she really enjoys it. She has no trouble at all keeping up with the work (perceptual defence).

VALUES AND BELIEFS

Values are the moral principles that guide the activities of a person or an organisation. They are extremely important in decision making because, without them, it would be impossible to evaluate different courses of action. Problems arise however, when the values of the individual clash with the values of the organisation as a whole. Quite often, managers have to put their personal values aside because they are required to support a policy or a decision with which they disagree.

For example, a manager who believes in looking after the workforce, may disagree with the decision to purchase new equipment that will make some of them redundant. Ironing out such incompatibilities is one of the reasons why many organisations are trying to bring their values into the open and to agree some shared values with the workforce.

Individuals' values tend to grow out of their beliefs about the world. Here are some popular expressions of beliefs on which value systems are based.

All individuals have the potential to excel at something.

There is life after death.

Nothing we can do will alter things.

People want to be winners.

When a number of similar beliefs are organised around a particular area of life, a **value system** starts emerging. Once value systems are established, they serve as a powerful force for influencing our judgements and our decisions. Our choice of career or path in life is often the first major decision we make that is coloured by our beliefs and values.

ACTIVITY 3

Use this activity to help you to identify your own values about work. Consider the values listed in the box below. Are these values:

1. very important?

2. important?

3. fairly important?

4. of little or no importance?

Tick the boxes headed 1, 2, 3 or 4 that apply to you.

Values	1	2	3	4
Planning and managing my own work				
Gaining recognition and status through my work				
Job security				
Good working conditions				
Getting on well with people I work with				
Doing work which helps me to learn new skills				
The chance of promotion and advancement				
Earning enough to live well				
Feeling I have achieved something worthwhile				
The chance to discover or try out new ideas				
Personal power and influence				
Fulfilling my potential				
A sense of belonging				
Working with people who support each other				
Working with people with a similar background to mine				
Doing work that involves a physical effort				

Commentary...

The values that you have identified as being 'very important' should find their expression in the type of career or work that you eventually decide on. These values will be an important influence when the time comes to evaluate various job or life opportunities and make a choice. In the same way, managers bring their personal value systems to bear when they make both important and routine organisational decisions.

The activity may have illustrated another important point about values: they are not always consistent. Different values can emerge as a result of particular circumstances. For example, if you have identified 'working with people' as a priority for you, the importance of this may diminish if a well-paid job is offered that involves working on your own most of the time. In this case, different values then start to impinge on the process of making a decision with more immediacy than your original criterion.

Most people are not consciously aware of the values that they bring to bear on the decision-making process. So it can be useful for people in business to identify and discuss their personal values and compare these with those of the organisation as a whole. In this way, they can make their values operate at a more conscious level, make them more consistent and improve the quality of their decision making accordingly.

The choice process

Once decision makers have generated a range of possible solutions or decisions, they finally have to choose the best option. A number of techniques can help them to choose the right one.

PROS AND CONS

This commonly used method involves listing the advantages and disadvantages of different courses of action, then choosing the one with the most advantages.

If, after completing the two lists the decision is still not clear, the next step is to weight the different ideas. Each one is weighted according to its importance, using a scale from one to ten; then the scores are added up and the highest total wins.

PROS AND CONS OF TAKING ON NEW STAFF

For two partners in a small business, trying to decide whether or not to take on a part-time administrative assistant, the pros and cons of the decision might look like this:

Pros:

- We will be free of the time-consuming, routine work (8).

- We will have more time to devote to the productive side of the business (7).

- An administrative assistant would have specialist bookkeeping skills which we do not have (5).

Cons:
- The regular pay cheque would be an additional overhead that the business might not be able to support indefinitely (9).

- We would have to devote time to induction training (4).

- It would be some time before the person was self-programming (6).

- We would have to provide office space and equipment for the new person (7).

You can easily see which side won in the above debate!

VOTING

This method is widely used when it is difficult to reach a consensus. However, it should only be used if everyone is prepared to be committed to the outcome.

TAKING A VOTE IN A MEETING
A group of managers is discussing the imminent introduction of a new computer system into their departments. The computers are to be networked, and it is important that staff training in all the departments should be done at roughly the same time.

Two of the managers are arguing over what they see as an important point. George thinks that the operators should be sent on an external training course and Julia is convinced that the training should be carried out in-house. The discussion continues for about ten minutes while the rest of the group listens fascinated as points are raised and hotly disputed on both sides.

Finally, just as it seemed that there is no way out of the impasse, someone suggests that the group should take a vote. Without hesitation, everyone but George votes for the in-house course.

CONSENSUS

To reach a consensus, a group should keep the discussion going until a mutually acceptable decision is reached. It relies on everyone being honest about their true feelings and opinions. A good group chairperson can usually make sure that all participants in the decision-making process have a chance to say what they think, and that none of them leaves the meeting feeling that a decision has been imposed without proper discussion and agreement.

CLUSTERING

This is a way of dealing with a large number of options, e.g. after a brainstorming session. The ideas are clustered into groups and each group is then evaluated separately. The advantage is that ideas can be combined or adapted without losing any of them.

SAT:
allow 15 mins

Managing tasks and solving problems ✓

ACTIVITY 4

Cluster these ideas for solving the problem of shoplifting in a chain of newsagents' shops:

- Install fake video cameras.

- Allow only three school children to enter at one time.

- Hire full-time 'plain clothes' security staff.

- Install a mechanism that locks the doors automatically if shoplifting is suspected.

- Train sales staff to identify shoplifters.

- Install real security cameras.

- Put prices up to compensate for stolen goods.

- Hire uniformed security staff to guard the shops at busy times.

- Ban known shoplifters from entry.

- Train sales staff in procedures for dealing with shoplifters.

- Monitor the situation but take no action.

- Ask the police to look in at times when it is known that shoplifting occurs.

- Pay a security firm to assess the situation and to come up with an integrated solution that can be used in all shops in the chain.

Commentary...

Here are the clusters that we decided upon. If yours are different, however, this does not means that they are wrong.

Using technology:

- ○ Install fake video cameras.
- ○ Install a mechanism that locks the doors automatically if shoplifting is suspected.
- ○ Install real security cameras.

Hiring expert help from outside:

- ○ Hire full-time 'plain clothes' security staff.
- ○ Hire uniformed security staff to guard the shops at busy times.
- ○ Pay a security firm to assess the situation and to come up with an integrated solution that can be used in all shops in the chain.

Training:

- ○ Train sales staff to identify shoplifters.
- ○ Train sales staff in procedures for dealing with shoplifters.

Quick and easy solutions:

- ○ Allow only three school children to enter at one time.
- ○ Put prices up to compensate for stolen goods.
- ○ Ban known shoplifters from entry.
- ○ Monitor the situation but take no action.
- ○ Ask the police to look in at times when it is known that shoplifting occurs.

PRIORITISING

Each proposal is scored in relation to several pre-set criteria. The scores are then totalled. If desired, different weights can be applied to each criterion.

CRITERIA FOR NEW PREMISES
A company planning to move its headquarters out of London has set the following basic criteria for the new premises:

1. They must be near a motorway turn off.

2. They must be within a five-mile radius of a mainline railway station.

3. House prices in the area must be at an acceptable level.

4. Annual rent/rates must not exceed X.

5. The building must be large enough to accommodate 60 members of staff.

6. There must be sufficient car parking for 80 cars.

7. The building must have space for a large meeting room/boardroom.

8. The building must incorporate space for kitchens and a staff dining room.

The option that meets most of the desired criteria is selected.

NEGOTIATION

This approach is often used in bargaining for pay rises and in the process of bidding for annual budgets. With this method for selecting a mutually acceptable option, losses in one situation are compensated by wins in another.

These questions are frequently used by managers as a checklist for preparing to negotiate a compromise:

- What do I want to achieve?

- What is my fallback position? How far am I prepared to compromise if necessary?

- What does 'the other side' want to achieve?

- How can I meet objections to my point of view?

The type of compromise that can be arrived at through a process of negotiation can mean that a situation where one side loses and the other side wins is turned into one where both sides are winners to some extent.

ACTIVITY 5

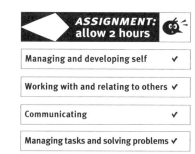

This assignment asks you to 'role play' the process of making a decision in a group of three or four. If you are working through this book on your own, you can still complete this assignment; however, rather than role playing the decision making process in a team, you should take the decisions on your own.

You are a manager in charge of a customer services department in a water company. The computer system that was installed two months ago allows team members to take on much more responsibility than was previously possible. They are now so efficient that they now require very little supervision. It is clear that the department can and should reduce costs by making one of its four team leaders redundant. You have called a management meeting to decide which one of these four people will be selected for redundancy:

- **Anna Knowles** has only been with the company for about six months. She is, however, well qualified and experienced and has already proved her efficiency as a worker and her effectiveness as a team leader. It has been a struggle for her to get and keep this job because she is a single parent and her child has a hearing and speech impairment.

- **Ben Stamford** is over fifty. He is well liked and respected in the department and, because he is an excellent worker, fair and level headed, he is frequently the one who holds everyone together in times of change or crisis. He knows the area and its people well because he has lived here all his life – this is quite an asset when dealing with irate customers. His wife is owner/manager of a company of marketing consultants.

- **Ravi Desai** seems to lack commitment to the job he is doing. There have been complaints from customers about his attitude and his sick absence record is one of the worst in the department. He claims that he is bored because he is capable of taking on a more responsible role, that his talents have not been valued and he has never been given a chance to apply for promotion. He has three small children under five.

- **Maureen O'Donnell** like Anna, is one of the department's most recent recruits. Maureen is very hardworking but, although she often works late or takes work home, she still finds it difficult to meet deadlines. She says that she has been overloaded with work and that she needs help in developing her self management skills. Maureen's husband was made redundant last year and she has three children of school age.

Use one of the methods described in this session to decide which of the four people on the shortlist will be made redundant.

Then, assume that water company's directors insist on further cuts.

You have to make one more team leader redundant. Use one of the other method's described in this session to choose between the three remaining team leaders.

Finally, write a report of about 1,800 words comparing the advantages and disadvantages of each of the methods you have chosen. Note your main points in the box below.

summary

▶ Before a final decision can made, decision makers have to make a 'shortlist' of suitable options and carry out an evaluation of these options.

▶ Three groups of evaluation criteria are commonly used: feasibility, acceptability and risk.

▶ Values are extremely important in decision making. Without them it would be impossible to 'evaluate' different courses of action. Problems arise however, when the values of the individual clash with the values of the organisation as a whole.

▶ Once decision makers have generated a range of possible solutions or decisions, they finally have to choose the best option. A number of techniques can help them to choose the right one: pros and cons, voting, consensus, clustering, prioritising and negotiation.

Contingency Planning

Identifying contingencies

WHY IS CONTINGENCY PLANNING IMPORTANT?

APPROACHES TO CONTINGENCY PLANNING

RECOGNISING CONTINGENCIES

Objectives

After participating in this session, you should be able to:

▶ explain the purpose and nature of contingency plans

▶ compare ad hoc and planned approaches to contingencies

▶ create simple scenarios for a specified industry

▶ identify the factors that might hinder an organisation's ability to achieve its objectives

▶ describe a range of forecasting techniques.

In working through this session, you will practise the following BTEC common skills:

Managing and developing self	✔
Working with and relating to others	✔
Communicating	✔
Managing tasks and solving problems	✔
Applying numeracy	
Applying technology	
Applying design and creativity	

Why is contingency planning important?

Life will never be easy, nor perfectible, nor completely predictable. It will be best understood backwards but we have to live it forwards. To make it liveable, at all levels, we have to learn to use the paradoxes, to balance the contradictions and the inconsistencies and to use them as an invitation to find a better way.

Charles Handy, 1995, *The Empty Raincoat*, Arrow Books

We have already looked at how managers tackle the complex processes of strategic and operational planning and decision making. These are the tools they use to develop the organisation in a desired direction, to consider the options that are open to them and to select the best strategy for current and future circumstances.

Unfortunately, things are never quite that straightforward. The turbulence of the Western economies during the 1980s and 1990s has confirmed the importance of contingency planning as a major tool in the planner's armoury.

> \!?/ **Contingency planning** is a technique that aims to reduce or eradicate uncertainty from strategic and operational planning.
> **Contingency plans** are attempts to answer the 'what if?' questions about major issues that can seriously affect an organisation and the achievement of its long-term success.

Managers do their best to think through their plans, but they cannot be certain that the actual outcomes will be the ones that they originally planned for. Organisations are constantly faced with a range of possible future developments in the internal and external environment. The price of raw materials might rise, consumers' demand for products might fall, competitors could implement an unexpected but damaging strategy, fulfilling an order might incur unexpected costs. Planning for contingencies means imagining the more likely 'what if?' situations, and then deciding what to do if these materialise.

Contingency plans can be made at any level:

- At the **strategic level** – for example, a company planning to expand into the overseas market may be uncertain about exchange rates or tariff barriers. In the event that exchange rates remain favourable or barriers come down, the strategic contingency plan could be to produce goods in the UK and export them. If, however, tariffs multiply or there appears to be a long-term increase in the value of the pound, the plan could be to set up a manufacturing operation abroad.

- At the **operational level** – for example, input costs may be much higher than expected, equipment or systems could break down or there may be unexpected loss or damage to products being manufactured. Many organisations have a 'contingency budget' to cope with unexpected costs. Having a good maintenance contract for machinery is another common operational contingency plan.

- At the **individual level** – most people make personal contingency plans to cope with events that threaten to alter their current lifestyle. If you have ever said things like 'What will I do if I lose my job?' or 'How will I cope if X dies?' or, more cheerfully, 'If I win a million pounds, how will I spend it?' then you are making contingency plans.

SECURING DATA AND SYSTEM SOFTWARE

One major contingency plan for most organisations is to ensure that data held on computer files is kept safe and free from contamination. An information system has to be protected against four main categories of risk:

- fraud

- theft

- wilful damage

- disasters like fire, flood and loss of power.

THE IMPORTANCE OF GOOD SECURITY
It is thought that UK companies lose about 1.5 billion a year from crime and other disasters and that one company in every thousand suffers a major failure in its computer systems each year. One major computer crash cost a bank 22 million in lost interest because it was unable to place customers' money in interest bearing overnight accounts. Most companies who are dependent on computer-based information systems will go under if they suffer a major system failure and have neglected to arrange for adequate back-up.
Source: Carol Cashmore and Richard Lyall, 1991, *Business Information Systems and Strategies*, Prentice Hall, p.246.

WHY IS CONTINGENCY
PLANNING IMPORTANT?

Achieving adequate computer security requires a great deal of planning and considerable financial investment. How much time and resources managers decide to invest depends on the level of risk involved and the consequences for the company of a failure in security.

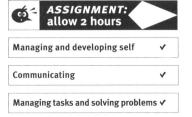

ASSIGNMENT: allow 2 hours	
Managing and developing self	✔
Communicating	✔
Managing tasks and solving problems	✔

ACTIVITY 1

Write a report, of approximately 1500 words, on the main systems that companies use for protecting their data and computer hardware against fraud, corruption and theft. You will need to undertake some research in the library and talk to some computer experts.

Make sure that, as a minimum, you discuss the following in your report:

- restriction of access to the system

- separation of duties

- passwords

- access logging systems

- minimising the risk of fire, flood and theft

- maintenance

- preparing back-up files.

Write your report on separate paper. Use the box below to make notes and to summarise your findings.

Approaches to contingency planning

When businesses have to cope with contingencies they can use one of two strategies. They can adopt an **ad hoc approach** – this means taking each event as it occurs and dealing with it there and then. Alternatively, they can adopt a **planned approach** – this involves trying to foresee contingencies and planning for them properly.

AD HOC APPROACHES

Ad hoc approaches to contingency are commonly used by small or medium sized businesses that do not see planning as an important priority. Larger organisations that do make contingency plans may still have to adopt a pragmatic approach when they are confronted by events that they have not foreseen.

Successful managers rely on being able to react effectively to sudden changes in the internal and external environment. It is impossible to anticipate everything that might occur to affect the organisation's carefully laid plans. Managers have to be pragmatic to cope with unexpected contingencies such as:

- in a single month two staff get married, two go down with 'flu and one breaks an ankle playing hockey

- a sudden stock market crash makes share prices plummet

- a competitor implements a novel and daring strategy that affects market share

- a scandal or an accident within the industry severely affects the image of the organisation's products.

**APPROACHES TO
CONTINGENCY PLANNING**

Thus contingency planning will frequently be required to cope with an event or situation that was not foreseen and which may never happen a second time. If this type of situation occurs managers will often need to think and plan both rapidly and creatively. In these circumstances, there may be no time to go through the fully fledged planning process – to consult others, gather information and so on. Managers may have to make a snap decision based on a swift analysis of the situation and on prior experience of the same types of circumstances. Members of the emergency services have to be capable of this type of contingency planning.

When there is more time to gather information and to consult others, an action plan can be developed to suit these unique circumstances. The manager could then develop a plan by going through the steps of the problem-solving / decision-making process that we looked at in section 2, session 1 of the module.

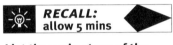

**RECALL:
allow 5 mins**

List the main steps of the
classic problem-solving
process.

Ad hoc planners may use many of the techniques we looked at in section 2 of the module to generate suitable options to cope with the contingency. The watchwords in this type of planning are **flexibility** and **speed**. In the rapidly changing organisational environment of the 1990s, managers often have to think and move faster than conventional planning approaches allow.

PLANNED APPROACHES

This is the converse of the *ad hoc* approach in that planning involves identifying all the major contingencies and working out what to do if those events occur. With a planned approach, it is possible to develop a number of different possibilities and plan for each of them. In this way, the organisation is ready for whichever eventuality actually materialises. The rest of this session and the next are devoted to the techniques and systems that organisations use to help them make these sorts of plans.

Although it may sound excellent in theory, there are some problems with the planned approach.

> **Contingency planning may work when the possibilities are circumscribed and each is well structured, based on long experience – as in the occurrence of snowstorms in northern cities or government interest rate changes affecting a bank. But contingency planning poses a problem in more open-ended contexts where knowledge about possible contingencies is limited.**
>
> Henry Mintzberg, 1994, *The Rise and Fall of Strategic Planning*, Prentice Hall

Mintzberg goes on to point out that, no matter how much time and expertise are invested in planning, the contingency that does occur may never have been identified. He also notes that contingency planning can cause 'paralysis by analysis'; in other words, managers are so busy foreseeing what might happen and planning for this that they have little time left to act.

Then there is the problem of managers feeling commitment to a contingency plan that they have devised. This is like the story of the Green Berets who were set up as a guerrilla force by the Pentagon before the Vietnam war 'just in case they were needed'. When the war started they made themselves needed – the contingency plan became a self-fulfilling prophecy. Here is Mintzberg again:

> **Of course, given pressures to act and a superficial understanding of a new situation, what more convenient response than to pull out the contingency plans at hand? They at least satisfy the leaders' need to do something and the planners' need to have been useful.**
>
> Henry Mintzberg, 1994, *The Rise and Fall of Strategic Planning*, Prentice Hall

Like most management processes, contingency planning should not be viewed as a panacea for all performance problems and planning failures. The human element, chance and coincidence all play their part in the success or otherwise of all types of organisational plans. Nevertheless, despite the reservations expressed by Mintzberg, many organisations feel that it is worth investing time and effort in trying to foresee the future and to cope with the most likely possibilities.

APPROACHES TO
CONTINGENCY PLANNING

SAT:
allow 10 mins

Managing tasks and solving problems ✔

ACTIVITY 2

Define and differentiate between *ad hoc* and planned approaches to contingency planning.

List the benefits of both approaches to contingency planning, and describe the problems of the planned approach.

Commentary...

Ad hoc contingency planning is a pragmatic approach in which each problem or event is dealt with when it occurs. A planned approach to contingency planning involves trying to foresee such problems and planning in advance how to deal with them.

The benefits of an *ad hoc* approach to contingency planning are that no time is wasted in planning for events that may never happen and each occurrence is dealt with as it occurs. In this way, it is possible to create a solution that is tailor-made for the particular circumstances.

Contingency planning helps organisations to deal with uncertainty and risk. Managers cannot hope that all their strategies will work out as planned because there are many variables in the internal and external environment that could have a bearing on the outcomes. Contingency planning is a technique that can make a major contribution to success in a turbulent business world.

The problems of contingency planning include:

- only being able to foresee the most obvious contingencies

- contingencies may not manifest themselves exactly as planned

- managers may spend too much time planning

- contingency plans may become self-fulfilling prophesies.

SCENARIO BUILDING

Scenario building is an approach to contingency planning that was first developed by Shell during the 1970s. Shell believed that the process would make decision makers more sensitive to signals of possible change in the world. They would then be able to respond more rapidly and effectively to change when it actually occurred.

Scenario building involves the identification of uncertainties, the factors that drive these and the formation of a range of possible assumptions about each one. The power of scenario building is that it depends less on formal analysis than on judgement. This is because scenarios focus on gaining an insight into the factors that contribute to outcomes rather than on forecasting outcomes.

To draw up scenarios, planners first consider the key forces that are to be developed into scenarios. Shell's experience has shown that it is best to restrict this analysis to the identification of environmental forces, rather than looking at the activities of competitors. This exercise then becomes a version of the PESTLE analysis discussed in section 1, session 4 of this module. The forces that Shell identified at this stage included:

- global concern for the environment

- war in the Middle East

- the discovery of new oil fields and the growth of Pacific Rim economies.

Next, planners have to attempt to understand the historical trend that is driving the assumptions under consideration. For instance, if they are examining the rise in oil prices, they need to develop a clear perception of the reasons why oil prices are increasing. This process will make their scenarios richer and more authentic.

At this point, different types of scenarios are created – often characterised by the titles **best case, worst case** or **dominant theme**. Planners aim to make their scenarios both logical and possible, and to keep the number of alternatives down to two or at the most four. It would be impossible to develop useful pictures for any more than that. An example of this is shown below.

SHELL'S GLOBAL SCENARIOS

In 1990, Shell's central planning group produced two scenarios entitled 'global mercantilism' and 'sustainable world'. The world at this time was seen in terms of three areas of potentially far-reaching change: geopolitics, international economics and the natural environment. These form a common starting point from which two different logic-flows branch towards the distinct scenarios. The branching point for these two stories is a (hypothetical) simultaneous economic downturn in several major countries.

Global mercantilism is the projected outcome of a weak international order as a result of the end of the Cold War. There is instability in the world's economic and political systems which leads to a focus on building a new, more managed regional system. The emphasis is on regional pacts and bilateral agreements rather than a global system. It encourages internal protectionist thinking within countries or blocs, but also recognises that companies need to be competitive. The route to competitiveness is seen to lie in a free-market approach so that deregulation and privatisation are the perception. Environmental concerns are not high on the political agenda in this picture; although local/regional actions may be taken, international environmental issues prove too difficult to resolve.

Here the energy industry faces changing rules and the continuous reconfiguration of markets. Regional self-sufficiency is the emphasis and non-OPEC production is continued. Oil marketeers and producers develop tight bonds and reciprocal arrangements while volatile economic growth makes it hard to control oil prices.

Sustainable world, in contrast, puts the environment at the top of the list. Political and economic thinking converge in a world where the importance of international trade agreements is recognised and pursued. Large economic powers, in particular, recognise that there are limits to the burden that can be placed on the environment, so there is a shift to tighter environmental regulation and taxation. This world has a global, caring outlook, with concern for developing countries and aid given to try to help achieve environmental impact. Pressure is exerted as regulation for lower emissions into the atmosphere and incentives to gain greater energy efficiency are introduced. The technology exists to meet the challenge, and economic conditions are made favourable so that, with time, the environmental pay-back is reaped.

Sources: *Challenge and Opportunities for the Petroleum Industry,* Shell, October 1991;
Global Scenarios for the Energy Industry, *Challenge and Response,* January 1991

ACTIVITY 3

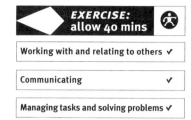

Working with and relating to others ✔

Communicating ✔

Managing tasks and solving problems ✔

In a group of three or four, build up a 'best case' and a 'worst case' scenario, each one starting with the words 'The government cuts duty on alcoholic drinks by 50 per cent ...'

Be as broad as possible in your thinking about the possible good and bad effects of the reduction in excise duty.

For example, your best case scenario may start: 'The government cuts duty on alcoholic drinks by 50 per cent and sales go up by 25 per cent in the space of six months. The increase in supermarket sales is particularly dramatic ...'

Your worst case scenario might start: 'The government cuts duty on alcoholic drinks by 50 per cent and sales triple almost immediately. However, vast numbers of pubs, clubs and bars may have to close down because ...'

Write your scenarios in the box below.

Commentary...

Here are our examples of scenarios on this theme, but yours may be very different from these.

Best case scenario

The government cuts duty on alcoholic drinks by 50 per cent and sales go up by 25 per cent in the space of six months. The increase in supermarket sales is particularly dramatic – with the largest rise being to the over 50s age group and the most popular items being wines and spirits. There is a social trend for this group to entertain at home rather than going out to the pub for a drink. Life has become very sociable and lively for many of them and sales of party snacks, indoor and outdoor games and home cinema systems have increased considerably.

The younger age groups frequent the numerous café style bars that have opened in high streets up and down the country. Some are continental style bars which are frequented by families who go to meet friends and enjoy a drink. Others are 'theme' bars – the Wild West, old Amsterdam, science fiction, virtual reality – where young people go to drink, dance and relax.

Worst case scenario

The government cuts duty on alcoholic drinks by 50 per cent and sales triple almost immediately. However, vast numbers of pubs, clubs and bars close down because people drink almost exclusively at home or in the street. The rate of alcoholism, alcohol-related diseases, crime and social problems has increased, stretching the services provided by health and social services, the police forces and voluntary organisations past their limits.

The government has to pour more funds into existing services and new ones have to be developed to meet emerging needs. One particularly regrettable consequence of cheaper alcohol is the incidence of alcoholism and liver diseases in the under-15 age group. Several hundred private detoxification clinics have opened up and a number of psychologists have dedicated their work to helping people to cure their alcohol addiction.

Recognising contingencies

So far, we have been emphasising the importance of the first step of the contingency planning process – that of identifying possible contingencies. Effective managers recognise that one of the most valuable keys to success here is simply being and remaining aware of what it is that makes their organisation 'tick'. If any of the innumerable factors that keep things running changes or disappears, this could have an adverse effect on performance or on the achievement of objectives.

A useful way of identifying contingencies is for managers to discuss the question: 'What does our success depend on?' When this question is answered it is then possible to imagine a potential situation, or range of situations, that might constrain this success. The task of setting up useful contingency plans is then made much easier to perform.

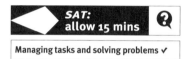

SAT:
allow 15 mins

Managing tasks and solving problems ✓

ACTIVITY 4

Imagine you a team leader in an organisation that manufactures computers for the aircraft industry. Do a brainstorm or a mind map of the factors on which it depends for its continued success.

Now extend the exercise by trying to imagine the factors that might remove or diminish each of these conditions.

Commentary...

Your list of factors which are important for the organisation's success may include some of the following:

- a stable, flourishing aircraft industry
- the ability to produce goods to the specification
- a reliable supply of components from different countries
- an effective research and development department
- good morale in the team
- effective managers
- satisfied customers
- a global economy that requires considerable business travel.

Factors which may diminish each of these conditions for success are in turn:

- defence cuts
- a lack of adequate resources
- components becoming more expensive or supply becoming unreliable
- an inappropriate culture, poor pay and conditions
- ineffective management recruitment and development procedures
- mistakes, or failure to supply orders on time
- a downturn in world economy.

Organisations use a number of techniques for identifying these types of contingencies, including **forecasting, research** and **judgement**.

FORECASTING

Forecasting allows managers to take a range of factors into account so as to predict what will happen more accurately. In particular, forecasting involves managers in:

- finding out and listening to what customers and stakeholders are saying about the organisation, its environment and the products and services it provides

- reflecting on their experience of what has happened in the past and assumptions about what is likely to happen

- drawing on other sources of information including their own records and published data

- looking for long-term trends.

Forecasting is a useful tool for managers because it can help them to design more reliable contingency plans. It will not, however, remove all the uncertainties.

Predictive forecasting involves examining recent records and using these to predict what will happen in the future. The technique is often used in operational plans to predict, say, next year's sales, equipment use or requirement for staff time. Basing one year's forecast on what happened the previous year works well when the situation is fairly stable. However, when the situation is volatile, managers need to be sure that there are no underlying trends or seasonal variations that may bias their forecasts. In this case, they can try two approaches:

1. **Comparing figures** for different years helps to distinguish seasonal variations from long-term trends. If information is presented on a graph, it can more easily be compared with what happened the year before, thus giving an idea of longer-term trends.

2. **Statistical techniques,** used correctly, can highlight such long-term changes and trends.

One of the main statistical approaches is **exponential smoothing**. This technique seeks to enhance predicitive accuracy by looking back at actual and forecast figures for previous periods and using the discrepancies between these figures to improve current forecasts. It applies a weighting system which allocates most importance to the data from the last period, slightly less to that from two periods ago and even less to that from three periods ago, and so on.

The first step is to calculate the difference between the forecast and the actual figures for each of the previous periods being examined. Each difference is then multiplied by a number, or 'weight', which is largest for the most recent period and smallest for the least recent. These weighted correction factors are then added to that forecast for the last period to give the forecast for the current period. The following example is merely a simplified illustration of the principle of this technique. Students should refer to any statistics textbook for a detailed explanation.

	Quarter 1	Quarter 2	Quarter 3
Actual sales	250	200	210
Forecast sales	230	185	225
Difference between actual and forecast	+20	+15	-15
Weighting factor	0.3	0.6	0.8
Weighted correction factor	+6	+9	-12

In this example, the total correction factor is 6 + 9 − 12 = 3. If the forecast for the current period is 250, the corrected forecast would be 250 + 3 = 253.

In certain situations, it might be appropriate to use **causal forecasting**. This would be the case if managers wanted to predict the impact of one factor on another. For example, a production manager may need to predict how many shifts will be needed over the next quarter if the company receives a particularly large order. He or she could check how many shifts were worked each month over the past year and compare this with the output for that month. It would then be possible to estimate how many shifts would be likely to meet the next quarter's expected demand.

Once again a graph can help to present this data more simply and statistical techniques are available as well. In particular, computer programs are available that enable managers to analyse data and produce forecasts.

RESEARCH

To make forecasting and contingency planning as accurate as possible, it is crucial to do some research using reliable information sources. Key sources include:

- opinions of managers, staff, customers, suppliers and experts in the field

- published data, e.g. government data such as demographic trends, or commercially available market data such as that produced by Euromonitor or Income Data Services

- journals, newspapers and books

- competitor analysis

- records of sales, productivity or performance.

Judgement

Using judgement in contingency planning is crucial – it can lead to some of the most inspired decisions an organisation can make. But it suffers from the fact that no one gets everything right all the time, and a wrong guess can prove costly in terms of wasted time and effort.

However, there are ways in which managers can improve the quality of their judgement. They can, for instance:

- keep themselves well informed and up to date with developments

- make the most of other people, inside and outside the organisation, who appear to make sound judgements

- use a team approach to prepare judgements and apply creative problem-solving processes.

Managers who work to develop their ability to make good judgements obtain valuable pay-offs in their contingency planning. All planning involves some judgement and, in some cases, there is little or no hard data available.

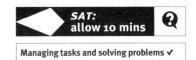

SAT:
allow 10 mins

Managing tasks and solving problems ✓

ACTIVITY 5

These people are talking about how they intend to identify contingencies.

Person 1: Getting that contract would have a big impact on the numbers of staff we need in production and distribution. Lets see if we can work out what extra capacity we shall need.

Person 2: Ask the sales force to make a point of talking to our customers out in the field over the next month. Then put their ideas together with your own and produce a report detailing some of the problems that might arise if we implement this new strategy.

Person 3: There's no time to get any more information on this but I'm sure we have enough experienced people in our team to identify the potential risks between us. Let's ask people to take time to think about it and then call a meeting.

Person 4: Before going ahead with this expansion, we need to find out what the forecast sales are for the next five years. Have a look at our performance over the past five years and give me some detailed figures.

Person 5: There could be real problems with borrowing that amount of money. If the pound falls and interest rates go up the whole project could be jeopardised. I'd better get our financial people to investigate the risks involved.

In each case, name the approaches (or combination of approaches) that they are proposing to adopt. Are they going to use predictive forecasting, causal forecasting, research or judgement?

Commentary...

You should have said that the approaches proposed to identify contingencies are:

1. causal forecasting

2. a combination of research and judgement

3. judgement

4. predictive forecasting

5. research.

summary

▶ Contingency plans are the 'what if?' plans made in preparation for the more likely major changes or factors which will seriously affect an organisation and the achievement of its long-term success.

▶ When businesses have to cope with contingencies they adopt either an *ad hoc* approach which means taking each event as it occurs, or a planned approach which involves trying to foresee contingencies and planning for them properly.

▶ Scenario building consists of the identification of uncertainties, the factors that drive these and the formation of a range of possible assumptions about each one.

▶ A useful way of identifying contingencies is for managers to discuss what the success of their business depends on. When this question is answered, it is possible to imagine a potential situation, or range of situations, that might constrain this success.

▶ Forecasting allows managers to take a range of factors into account so as to predict what will happen more accurately. Predictive forecasting involves examining recent records and using these to predict what will happen in the future. Causal forecasting means predicting the impact of one factor on another.

▶ Managers who develop their ability to make good judgements obtain valuable pay-offs in their contingency planning.

Coping with risk

Objectives

After participating in this session, you should be able to:

⬇

> ▶ analyse the probability and effects of different types of risk

⬇

> ▶ identify and describe types of decision models

⬇

> ▶ construct a simple decision tree

⬇

> ▶ identify different ways of dealing with contingencies.

In working through this session, you will practise the following BTEC common skills:

Managing and developing self	✔
Working with and relating to others	
Communicating	✔
Managing tasks and solving problems	✔
Applying numeracy	
Applying technology	
Applying design and creativity	

Risk analysis

All strategies, no matter how well they have been evaluated, are prone to risk. Risk is usually analysed in terms of a range of possible outcomes or contingencies. Contingency planning can enable other strategies to be devised to deal with the various types of risk.

A valuable way of anticipating the kind of things that can go wrong is to think about the potential areas of concern in the strategic or operational plans that have been selected for implementation.

The main categories of risk can be summarised as follows:

- Physical risk
- Input risk
- Technical risk
- Labour risk
- Political and social risk
- Liability risk
- Outcome risk

Physical risk is the risk that there will be loss of or damage to equipment, buildings or information as a result of accident, fire or natural disaster.

Input risk is the risk that supplies or raw materials will not be available when they are required. Input risk also includes shortage of finance, information and human resources.

Technical risk is the risk that a new system will not work, or that it will not work well enough to deliver the anticipated benefits, or that there will not be enough people with necessary expertise to make it work satisfactorily.

Labour risk is the risk that key people will be unable to contribute to the strategy because of illness, career development opportunities, industrial action, and so on.

Political and social risk is the risk that the strategy will be impaired as a result of a change of government, the actions of the local council, or because of a shift in policy, or in response to protests from the community, the media, customers or members of staff (perhaps through their unions).

Liability risk is the risk that the strategy will be undermined through legal action (or the threat of it), because some aspect of it is arguably illegal, or because of insurance claims or claims for compensation if something goes wrong.

Outcome risk is the risk that products or services may turn out to be inadequate, leading to a negative impact on customers and stakeholders.

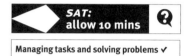

SAT:
allow 10 mins

Managing tasks and solving problems ✔

ACTIVITY 1

The management team of a sports centre is planning to try to increase the use of its facilities during the week by providing a crèche for children under five. Here are some of the things that they think might go wrong with the plan – categorise them in terms of the above groups.

1. There may be insufficient take up of the crèche facility.

2. Social services may put up legal barriers.

3. We may get insurance claims if children injure themselves.

4. We may not be able to find the money to finance the crèche.

5. Having a lot of children around may cause additional wear and tear on the premises.

6. We may not be able to open the crèche for all the hours that people require it.

7. The play group next door may object to us setting up in competition.

8. We've never done this before – maybe we don't know enough to make the créche a success.

Commentary...

You probably categorised the risks as follows: (1) outcome risk (although services are not necessarily inadequate because of low take-up), (2) political and social risk, (3) liability, (4) input, (5) physical, (6) outcome, (7) political and social, and (8) technical risk.

THE LIKELIHOOD OF PROBLEMS AND THEIR EFFECTS

When such potential problems have been identified, the next step is to decide how likely it is that they will actually happen, and what impact they will have if they do happen. Managers find a matrix like the one illustrated in figure 2.1 helpful in making this assessment.

Potential adverse effect

	High	Low
High		
Low		

(Level of risk and/or uncertainty)

FIGURE 2.1: *The risk/adverse impact assessment matrix.*
SOURCE: Bill Richardson and Roy Richardson, 1992, *Business Planning: An Approach to Strategic Management*, 2nd edn, Pitman Publishing

This tool is designed to help planners to assess the relative adverse effects and levels of risk and uncertainty of aspects of their strategies. Here, risk is taken to mean the probability of a particular eventuality actually occurring. Although, as we shall see, this risk can be measured mathematically, subjective judgements are also frequently made.

This is how planners should interpret the matrix:

- If any elements are placed in the **top left-hand corner** this means that the event is highly likely to happen and that the consequence will be severe. Because of this, the overall strategy is a risky one.

- If any elements are placed in the **bottom left-hand corner** this means that although the event is not likely, the adverse effects are still very high so it may be worth reconsidering the strategy.

- If any elements are placed in the top or bottom **right-hand corners** this means that, even if there is a good chance that they will happen, the adverse consequences will not be serious.

Managing tasks and solving problems ✔

ACTIVITY 2

Assess the likelihood and the effects of the risks identified above. To start you off, here is our assessment of the first three.

1. There may be insufficient take up of the crèche facility: low risk, high adverse effects.

2. Social services may put up legal barriers: high risk, medium adverse effects.

3. We may get insurance claims if children injure themselves: high risk, high adverse effects.

Now plot all the risks on to the matrix in the box below.

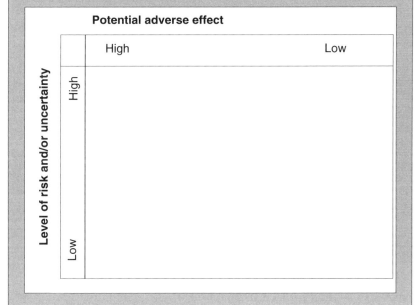

Commentary...

Your completed chart should look something like figure 2.2.

Potential adverse effect

FIGURE 2.2: *Completed risk/adverse impact assessment matrix.*

This sort of risk analysis is useful for planners because it draws their attention not only to the things that could go wrong with their plans but also to the probability of those things happening and their impact on the success of the plan as a whole. Thus, the process of carrying out the analysis is almost more important than its outcome.

ASSESSING PROBABILITY

One implication of the last activity is that a key skill in risk analysis is the ability to assess probability – the likelihood that something will happen. **Objective probability** requires that the likelihood of an occurrence be assessed on a basis which is independent of the person doing the assessment. For example, the managers of the sports centre could make a more objective assessment by investigating the outcomes of other projects of the same kind in a similar environment.

Subjective probability, on the other hand, relies on the personal beliefs of the assessor that a particular event will occur. Most people assess probability subjectively by searching through their personal experience for previous occurrences of similar events. But our memory of experiences may not provide a good guide to reality because we are influenced by our perceptions and our beliefs. As we saw in section 2, session 4 of this module, these factors can differ radically from individual to individual.

Our personal assessment of probability is influenced by a number of factors, each of which may be a source of bias in our judgements:

- **Vividness** – if you were in a car crash last week, you would almost certainly believe that the same event is highly likely to happen again. But this assessment is totally unrepresentative of the objective probability of the experience re-occurring.

- **Organisation** – the ability to recall depends to a great extent on how the memory is organised. For example, if you write about an experience in an organised way you are more likely to be able to remember it and use it to make judgements about probability.

- **Representativeness** – if you believe that an event is representative of previous judgements or situations, you are more likely to apply those same rules to make judgements in the future. For example, if a business is planning to take out a loan to buy a new piece of equipment, managers may judge that this is a low risk if they have had no trouble paying the interest on loans in the past. The problem is that the representativeness may not actually exist. This loan could be to finance a new type of contract, whereas previous ones may not have represented such a venture into unknown territory.

- **Reference points** – we are usually more prepared to offer a judgement if we can find a reference point against which to measure the situation. Many people are happier to wait for someone else to express an opinion before they give their own. And if that person is someone we have often agreed with in the past, we may concur with their judgement without proper thought.

We now examine some of the more sophisticated tools and techniques which can help managers to analyse risks.

Decision modelling

Decision modelling is an approach which seeks to overcome the subjectivity of different individual perceptions of a problem or situation. A decision model is a clear picture that summarises the various elements contributing to a decision which has to be made. It is a way of coping with uncertainty by organising and formalising the information about that decision.

Decision models can take many forms:

- flow charts

- network diagrams

- decision trees

- spreadsheets

- matrices.

They can be computerised or drawn and calculated manually.

An effective model will depend on the planner's understanding of the parameters and variables that have a bearing on the decision and of the cause and effect pattern of influence between the variables. The **parameters** are the factors that will not, and cannot, change during the lifetime of the decision being made.

The variables in a decision model can be **controllable** (factors which the decision maker has the power to change) or **uncontrollable** (factors which are controlled by the decision environment). Variables can also be placed in the categories of **inputs** (the decision options) and **outputs** (the consequences of the decision).

Thus, in any decision model, you may have controllable or uncontrollable inputs or controllable or uncontrollable outputs. The model itself draws out the pattern of cause and effect, showing how the input factors influence the output factors.

Cook and Slack provide an example of a simple decision model called a **cause and effect diagram** (figure 2.3). This decision model for part of the stock control decision is arrived at by working backwards from the output variables:

- The output variable 'total ordering cost' is determined by the cost of making an order together with 'order frequency'.

- The order frequency is, in its turn, a function of demand rate and 'order quantity', both input variables.

So, the total ordering cost depends partly on the fixed costs to the organisation of making an order and the variable costs related to numbers and rate of orders received.

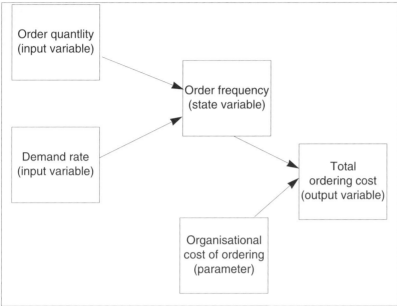

FIGURE 2.3: *Cause and effect diagram.*
SOURCE: Cook and Slack, 1991, *Making Management Decisions,* 2nd edn,
Englewood Cliffs, NJ, Prentice Hall

RECALL:
allow 5 mins

Before moving on, define for yourself the different aspects of a decision model. Complete these sentences:

○ **Parameters are ...**

○ **Controllable inputs are ...**

○ **Uncontrollable inputs are ...**

○ **Controllable outputs are ...**

○ **Uncontrollable outputs are ...**

Models are not just useful in helping managers to identify the best decision option, they are also valuable for making their thinking processes more systematic and creative and for improving their understanding of both the factors that have a bearing on a decision and the possible outcomes of a particular decision.

We now look at two more sophisticated forms of decision modelling used in contingency planning – sensitivity analysis and decision trees.

SENSITIVITY ANALYSIS

Sensitivity analysis is a valuable technique for predicting contingencies and assessing risk. It has proved to be an excellent way of drawing out uncertainties and communicating them to planners, although it does not actually make a choice or a decision for them.

The use of sensitivity analysis has increased with the development of computerised spreadsheets which lend themselves especially well to this type of application. The technique enables managers to identify, challenge and change any of the assumptions that lie behind a particular strategy. Its most valuable benefit is that it can test how sensitive the expected performance is to each of these assumptions.

For example, if a key assumption of a particular strategy is that demand will increase by 10 per cent, sensitivity analysis asks what the effect on profitability would be if the market grew by only 5 per cent. If a key assumption is that the value of the pound will remain stable, the program will analyse the effects of a fall or a rise in the value of the pound. Managers can then use their judgement to decide if they should alter their plans in the light of the outcomes of the analysis.

DECISION TREES

Decision trees break down large decisions into smaller steps. The possible outcomes of those small decisions are then represented by the branches of a tree.

In the simplified example shown in figure 2.4, a decision tree is used to assist a company in its strategic planning. There are eight directions that the company might pursue, each one depending on a different combination of decision variables. The decision tree analyses the effects of the key elements that development options are intended to incorporate. In this case the company's managers have asked the following three questions:

1. Do we want high growth or no growth?

2. Do we want high or low investment?

3. Do we want to diversify – yes or no?

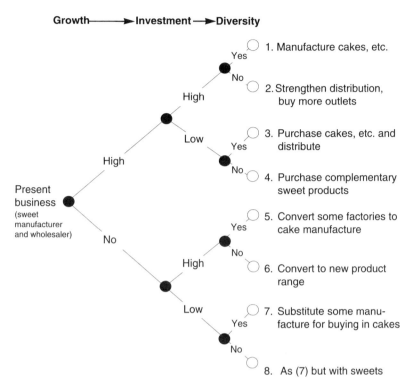

Growth ──────► Investment ──► Diversity

FIGURE 2.4: *A simplified decision tree.*
SOURCE: Johnson, G. and Scholes, G., 1993, *Exploring Corporate Strategy*,
Englewood Cliffs, NJ, Prentice Hall, p.275

SAT:
allow 10 mins

Managing tasks and solving problems ✔

ACTIVITY 3

Use the information in the decision tree in figure 2.4 to answer the following questions:

○ Which four options would take priority if choosing growth is an important part of the company's future strategy?

○ Which four options would rank highest if low investment is important?

○ Which four options would the company consider if it did not want to diversify?

Commentary...

If choosing growth is an important part of the company's future strategy, options 1–4 would take priority over options 5–8.

If low investment is important, options 3, 4, 7 and 8 would rank highest.

If the company did not want to diversify, options 2, 4, 6 and 8 would be the ones to consider.

The decision tree approach makes it possible to identify at least the major alternatives and the fact that later decisions may depend on how current decisions work out in the end. By incorporating probabilities of various events in the tree, it is possible to understand the real probability of a decision leading to the desired results. What may have seemed to be the best idea at the beginning may start to look quite risky when a decision tree is applied. At the very least, decision trees focus on the important elements in a decision and bring assumptions and reasoning processes out into the open.

Dealing with contingencies

As discussed in the previous session, the purpose of contingency planning is to generate a range of responses to identified potential situations. Organisations use a range of strategies for coping with uncertainty, e.g.:

- looking for more information
- hedging your bets
- doing something completely different
- going full steam ahead
- doing nothing
- devising detailed contingency plans.

LOOKING FOR MORE INFORMATION

In some circumstances, particularly where the organisation is dealing with a high degree of uncertainty, it makes sense to gather more information before making any important decisions. However, collecting information is itself expensive and time consuming, so the cost of this process needs to be weighed against its anticipated benefits. Contingency plans that are made in a hurry because there is no time to gather information can be especially risky.

Making decisions without adequate information is often disastrous. In retrospect, the Channel Tunnel is a good example of an enterprise that went ahead without adequate information or contingency planning. Some of the difficulties experienced by the project both during the lengthy construction period and its first year of operation may have been avoided if more information had been available and if more appropriate contingency plans had been made.

If a decision is an important one, time should be invested in collecting and interpreting good quality information. We discussed the significance of information for decision making in section 2, session 2 of this module.

HEDGING YOUR BETS

This is the process of modifying existing plans now to protect against possible contingencies in the future. A good example is when you take out insurance just in case you are burgled, your car is stolen or your house catches fire. Hedging involves foreseeing what might happen and building safeguards into the organisation's plans. Common examples of operational strategies which allow organisations to hedge their bets include:

- training people in first aid in case there is an accident at work

- signing up with an agency so that there is a ready supply of temporary staff in case a 'flu epidemic breaks out at times of peak demand

- taking out insurance in case the works syndicate wins the national lottery

- buying a generator in case of power failure

- investigating new developments in technology in case the organisation needs to buy in new equipment at short notice.

Efficient hedging requires accurate forecasting and good judgement based on experience and an awareness of trends.

DOING SOMETHING COMPLETELY DIFFERENT

If a particular contingency threatens the success of the whole enterprise, planners have to be aware that more than one route is open to them. They can use problem-solving or creative-thinking techniques to create a way forward that is less risky.

When the Eastern European markets started to open up in the early 1990s, a clothing company considered the option of targeting markets in Poland and the former East Germany. In the event, however, it drew back from this strategy because it considered that a German competitor's superior local knowledge would put the company at a substantial disadvantage. Instead it decide to consolidate its operation in the UK, targeting the niche markets of outdoor and indoor workwear.

GOING FULL STEAM AHEAD

Yet another possibility is to go ahead with the plan or the decision despite the risks, judging that circumstances will probably change anyway. Some people might consider this strategy to be robust entrepreneurship; others would call it foolhardy recklessness. The problem is that you never know whether this has been the right strategy until you can see if it has been successful or not.

THE ARTS CENTRE
A local council was criticised for its decision to go ahead and build a £5 million arts centre on the edge of the South Wales valleys in the midst of a recession. It was felt that the massive investment would never be recouped because people simply did not have the money to spend on activities such as concerts, theatre, exhibitions and arts workshops. It was also felt that people who had grown up in a culture of television and drinking would never be interested in more refined leisure pursuits. When the centre was completed it happened to coincide with a growing social need for a community meeting place and an interest in the performing arts among some groups of young people. After its first year, the centre was pronounced an overwhelming success and the council was congratulated for its vision in providing it.

DOING NOTHING

This strategy is often the riskiest one of all, especially in a business environment of constant change. Many businesses have disappeared because they believed, quite falsely, in some sort of mythical stability. They felt sure that, in the long term, the threat would disappear. We can cite the example of the village shop that does nothing when customers start using the big supermarket in the local town. If the shopkeeper does nothing to tempt people back, he or she will soon go out of business.

DEVISING DETAILED CONTINGENCY PLANS

These plans are schedules of activities that will be brought into action if a particular contingency arises. Planners will use the same processes and techniques discussed in section 1 of the module.

Good examples of contingency plans are those devised by local authority emergency planning officers. All local authorities are required by law to have contingency plans ready to put into action in the event of likely contingencies such as:

- train crashes

- multiple accidents on a motorway

- floods

- chemical leaks from manufacturing plants or spillages during transportation

- a nuclear disaster.

Every local authority has emergency contingency plans for eventualities that may be common to all areas, such as nuclear disasters or adverse weather conditions. But the nature of other contingency plans will depend on factors such as the geographical location of the area or the types of factories or other facilities that are sited within it. Thus, for example:

- local authorities situated on the edge of the sea or a river will probably have contingency plans to be implemented in case of flooding

- local authorities situated near large airports will have contingency plans to cope with aircraft crashes

- local authorities situated in the vicinity of chemical works will have plans made for action to take in the event of chemical leaks.

Each of these plans will involve the local authority in liaising with relevant agencies: the emergency services, the Inspectorate of Pollution, the National Rivers Authority, the Territorial Army, managers of local companies and so on. And the plans will probably incorporate:

- a goal and/or objectives

- strategies

- the roles and responsibilities of the organisations involved.

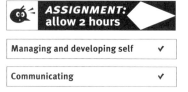

Managing and developing self ✔

Communicating ✔

Managing tasks and solving problems ✔

ACTIVITY 4

The aim of this assignment is to work through the processes involved in producing a contingency plan. You will be required to use some of the tools introduced in this session to develop an outline contingency plan.

First, choose both an organisation and a scenario that you want to investigate. You might want to choose a scenario that relates to your place of work or study. Or you might choose an example which allows you to use your imagination, say:

- a tour operator planning how to deal with an earthquake or revolution on a tropical island

- a hospital planning how to respond to a local transport disaster involving multiple casualties

- a railway company planning how to minimise disruption caused by severe weather conditions.

Find out as much information as you can about your chosen company and scenario. Organisations are unlikely to release details of their contingency plans but they may help you with background information. If you are studying at college, you might invite a local authority emergency planning officer to come and talk to you and others in the Business Studies group. If no planning officer is available, you could try:

- a member of the police force or fire brigade

- a manager from the regional electricity, gas or water company

- a manager from a local chemical plant, nuclear power station or similar manufacturing plant that uses potentially dangerous processes

- a manager from the nearest NHS Trust.

Once you have obtained as much information as possible, start to plan how your organisation might deal with the specific emergency or disaster. Develop a spider diagram and use decision tree techniques.

When you have concluded your investigation, write a report of 1,500 words that describes the strategies that have been devised to deal with the identified contingency. Your report should answer the following questions:

- Which contingency does this plan set out to cope with?

- What are the likely consequences of the contingency if no action is taken?

- What are the expected sequences of events?

- What are the objectives of your plan?

- What strategies have you selected for coping with this contingency?

- Who would be involved in implementing the strategy?

- What would their roles be?

- Which material resources (vehicles, medical supplies, sandbags) would be used to implement the plan?

- Comment on how effective you feel this plan would be in dealing with the particular contingency.

Write your report on separate sheets of paper. Use the box below for notes and to summarise your main findings.

summary

▶ Risk is usually analysed in terms of the range of possible outcomes or contingencies.

▶ When potential problems have been identified, the next step is to decide how likely it is that they will actually happen, and what impact they will have if they do happen.

▶ Objective probability requires that the likelihood of an occurrence is assessed on a basis which is independent of the person doing the assessment. Subjective probability depends on the personal belief of the planner that a particular event will occur.

▶ Decision models are necessary because each person's perception of a problem or a situation is unique. A model is a clear picture that is used to represent the various aspects of a decision which has to be made.

▶ Sensitivity analysis is a technique for predicting contingencies and assessing risk. It has proved to be an excellent way of drawing out uncertainties and communicating them to planners – it does not actually make a choice or a decision for them.

▶ Decision trees are a method of assessing risk by breaking down decisions into smaller steps. What happens is that the possible outcomes of those small decisions are represented by the branches of a tree.

▶ Organisations use a range of strategies for coping with uncertainty including: looking for more information, hedging your bets, doing something completely different, going full steam ahead, doing nothing or devising detailed contingency plans.

Resources

Resources

The pioneers who put people first

People Management

10 August 199

First Direct was founded in 1989 and is the largest telephone banking operation in the UK, with more than 500,000 customers (increasing by I0,000 a month) and 750,000 accounts. It is an autonomous division of Midland Bank plc, which is itself a member of the Hong Kong & Shanghai Banking Corporation Group.

Its 2,000 staff are all based at two sites in Leeds. They provide a round-the-clock service, 365 days a year. Although First Direct does not have to maintain a branch network, it subsidises the cost of its 20,000 calls a day from customers, who pay only the local rate from anywhere in the UK.

Kevin Newman, aged 38, took two degrees in government and politics before joining Mars Group in 1980 and training as a systems analyst. From 1985 to 1989 he worked on business systems and management information systems for Woolworths plc. He was then headhunted to join Midland Bank as part of the project team preparing for the launch of First Direct, becoming the new company's first IT director, then operations and IT director, deputy CEO and, from October 1991, chief executive.

First Direct has about 40 people in personnel and another 60 trainers. Newman thinks of employees either as 'profit generators' – those directly serving customers – or 'those who improve tomorrow's profit'. In more product-orientated businesses, he says, R&D and marketing are often seen as the most important future profit generators.

Newman believes that in banking, the HR and IT functions are equally as important. Investing in these, he says, is the main means of finding opportunities to save on costs and/or generate more profit.

Fisons picks up the gauntlet

The Guardian

4 September 1995

Fisons, the drugs group, will hit back at suggestions that it is preparing to surrender its independence and launch a fightback against the hostile £1.7 billion bid from Rhone-Poulenc Rorer, the US arm of France's chemicals conglomerate. Its defence document, to be published this morning, will be 'quite feisty', according to an insider and show the group as 'far from giving in'.

But Fisons is unlikely to pull any new money-spinning wonder-drugs out of the hat despite reports yesterday of a surprise in the document. Rather it will restate its belief in the underlying value of its respiratory medicine-delivery technology. The group is pulling out all the stops to convince share holders that it has a sound future as an independent company; Rhone-Poulenc Rorer has suggested that, by over-reliance on the marketing of other people's medicines, Fisons is pursuing a defunct strategy. It expects Fisons share price to drift this week as the weakness of the defence becomes clear. But the UK's fourth largest pharmaceuticals firm is thought likely to accuse RPR in turn of trying to cash in on the asthma scare that has gripped the industrial world by bidding low for a company with an international lead in delivery systems for respiratory medicines.

It will point out that – contrary to reports – it has not sold the whole of its research and development arm, the unit dealing with asthma and other breathing difficulties remains within the company. But there is likely to be no immediate indication of a 'white knight' rival bidder or merger partner nor any dramatic drug developments in the pipeline.

It has been the apparent absence of new medicines to replace the ageing anti-asthma drug, Intal, and its successor, Tilade, that has fuelled speculation that Fisons has no future on its own. Fisons is instead likely to restate its conviction that its lead in respiratory medicines gives it a flying start in the emergent new field of drugs for other illnesses that can reach the bloodstream through the lungs, rather than via the stomach or by needle injection.

Fisons says it has never ruled out agreeing to an offer it believes would value properly the company's respiratory technology, a willingness to deal underlined by the reputed 888,000 share options held by its new-broom chief executive, Stuart Wallis, the man credited with transforming Fisons into a group worth bidding for in the first place. The potential merger is likely to be approved by the European Commission and the offer has completed the pre-merger notification required under American monopolies laws.